Modern Greek Writers

Princeton Essays in
European and Comparative Literature

1. *The Orbit of Thomas Mann.*
By Erich Kahler

2. *On Four Modern Humanists:*
Hofmannsthal, Gundolf,
Curtius, Kantorowicz.
Edited by Arthur R. Evans, Jr.

3. *Flaubert and Joyce:*
The Rite of Fiction.
By Richard D. Cross

4. *A Stage for Poets: Studies in*
the Theatre of Hugo and Musset.
By Charles Affron

5. *Hofmannsthal's Novel* Andreas.
By David Miles

6. *Kazantzakis and the Linguistic*
Revolution in Greek Literature.
By Peter Bien

7. *Modern Greek Writers.*
Edited by Edmund Keeley and Peter Bien

Edited by Edmund Keeley and Peter Bien

MODERN GREEK WRITERS

SOLOMOS

CALVOS

MATESIS

PALAMAS

CAVAFY

KAZANTZAKIS

SEFERIS

ELYTIS

Princeton University Press

L.C. Card: 78-166379
I.S.B.N. 0-691-06215-3

Publication of this book has been aided by a grant from the Whitney Darrow Publication Reserve Fund of Princeton University Press

This book has been composed in Linotype Granjon

Printed in the United States of America by Princeton University Press, Princeton, New Jersey

In Memoriam

Benjamin Jackson

Acknowledgment

The Editors wish to express their gratitude to Professors C. A. Trypanis, Cedric Whitman, and Robert Fagles for their assistance in organizing this collection. They also wish to thank the following for their contribution to the English versions of one or more of the three essays (by Lorenzatos, Terzakis, and Vitti) that were originally written in Greek: Andonis Decavalles, George Giannaris, Mary Keeley, Julia Loomis, and Philip Sherrard.

Contents

Modern Greek Writers

Introduction

WE are all intrigued, perhaps mystified, by the way various nations suddenly blossom forth artistically. Poets, painters, and musicians whom we call great are so often just the most distinguished figures of a general artistic ferment usually centered in a single city or region and very clearly having a growth, peak, and decline. Athens in the Golden Age, Florence at the time of Dante, the London of Shakespeare, the Vienna of Mozart and Beethoven, the Paris of the Impressionists, Emerson's Boston, and the Dublin of Yeats and Joyce are diverse examples, all of which have been studied and admired throughout the West.

Although an equally extraordinary cultural flowering occurred in modern Greece, centered in Athens, unfortunately it has not been examined to the same degree, especially outside Greece itself. Indeed, until very recently the Greek literary renaissance has remained almost unknown even to those who consider themselves experts in European letters. The reason for this is the status of modern Greek as an "unimportant" language, an impediment that has been counteracted only minimally by the increase in translations; the swelling numbers of students who are learning the language in order to read Cavafy, Seferis, Kazantzakis, Palamas, and others in the original; and the small band of classically trained Hellenists who are extending their interests to Byzantium and the *tourkokratia*, realizing that not only the Greek language but also Greek literature has had an uninterrupted history stretching from Minoan times to the present.

A sense of modern Greece's cultural importance, a concern over the relative absence of coordinated scholarly attention to her achievements, and a hope that these might be made accessible to a much wider public led a group of American scholars to found the Modern Greek Studies Association. They were encouraged in this by the brilliant contributions of previous scholars, both Greek and European, and by continuing work in centers such as Geneva, Rome, London, Cambridge, Oxford, Birmingham, Chicago, Princeton, Cincinnati, and Montreal—not to mention Athens and Thessaloniki. They wished in particular to coordinate existing efforts; to stimulate further activity, especially in North America; and to see that more scholarly and critical material became available in English, the twentieth-century *koine*. In sum, the founders sought to provide for modern Greek language, literature, and history the services given other disciplines by existing associations of a similar nature.

The actual beginning of the MGSA (as it is known in abbreviated form) had a large element of the spontaneous in it. The idea emerged initially from an informal meeting of American scholars who came together in the fall of 1967 to plan a symposium on modern Greek literature under the sponsorship of the Comparative Literature Department at the University of Maryland.[1] The symposium that was held the following spring—undoubtedly the first such gathering in the Western hemisphere and probably the first anywhere in the world—proved to be a warm and stimulating occasion (although somewhat casually organ-

[1] Among those attending this meeting, called by Professor K. Mitsakis (then Acting Chairman of the Comparative Literature Department at Maryland), were Andonis Decavalles, Kostas Kazazis, Edmund Keeley, John Nicolopoulos, and Byron Tsangadas.

ized, since the various papers were not united by a central theme).[2] The planners of this symposium were so delighted to see how many others shared their enthusiasm for modern Greek literature, and so determined that the momentum achieved should not die at the symposium's end, that a small group of them joined several of the leading participants in forming a provisional executive committee which charged itself with the task of shaping the Association.[3]

The next step was to draft a constitution stating details of membership, administration, finances and, above all, purposes. The latter were articulated in this document as follows:

1. The general purpose shall be the fostering and advancement of modern Greek studies, particularly in the United States.

2. Toward this end, the association deems as its specific

[2] On the first day Basil Laourdas, visiting from Thessaloniki, surveyed the novels of Pandelis Prevelakis; A. O. Aldridge spoke on "Kazantzakis and the Modern Spirit"; and Kimon Friar, another visitor from Greece, roused the audience with his account of Kazantzakis' *Odyssey*. The second day offered studies of Cavafy's mythology and his position in the diaspora by John Anton and Basil Christides, respectively, and a survey of Kosmas Politis' novels by Andonis Decavalles. On the final evening, Edmund Keeley spoke on the "mythical method" in the poetry of Seferis. The program ended movingly with a talk on "Modern Greek Literature: a Quest for Identity," by Benjamin Jackson of the State Department, who was already visibly affected by the disease that was soon to kill him.

[3] The provisional executive committee consisted of John Anton, Peter Bien, Andonis Decavalles, Thomas Doulis, Mary Gianos, Edmund Keeley (Chairman), K. Mitsakis, John Nicolopoulos (Secretary), Byron Tsangadas, and Peter Topping.

purposes (a) to organize scholarly symposia in the various fields of modern Greek studies; (b) to finance, edit, and publish a professional journal; (c) to compile an annual bibliography of publications relating to modern Greek literature, culture, history, etc.; (d) to assist in establishing chairs, programs, and departments of modern Greek in American universities; (e) to encourage the teaching of modern Greek language, literature, and culture at all levels; (f) to serve as a center for the dissemination of literature and information regarding courses, books, and professional opportunities in the field of Byzantine and modern Greek studies, including literature, language, history, political science, and all other aspects of Greek civilization; (g) to support other groups and individuals sharing an interest in the realization of the above goals; (h) to encourage the formation within the Association of sections covering the various academic disciplines, such sections to be coordinated by secretaries elected by their membership; (i) to engage in any and all other activities as may be deemed necessary or expedient for the better realization of any of the foregoing purposes.

Some of these specific purposes are more visionary than others. To endow professorial chairs, for example, requires vast sums of money. Unsuccessful campaigns in the past have led the Association to feel that it should concentrate at first on realizable goals. Its initial action, therefore, was to establish an annual bibliography. This was made possible by affiliation with the Modern Language Association of America (MLA), in turn an affiliate of the American Council of Learned Societies (ACLS), and by the good fortune of securing the services of Mrs. Evro Layton, a trained librarian formerly in charge of the modern Greek collection at Harvard.[4] The bibliography will continue to be published in PMLA each June, and it should prove an indispensable resource for anyone interested in modern Greek studies. As an additional service in this general area, the Association is sponsoring a cooperative project to encourage and facilitate libraries in the purchase of books and journals printed in the Greek language. Under the terms of the project, Mrs. Layton selects items, orders them, and supplies cataloguing data, all according to the individual needs of subscribing institutions.[5]

A second realizable goal to which the Association turned its immediate attention was the organizing of meetings where scholars could present papers and discuss aspects of modern Greek culture. A seminar was established in connection with the annual December convention of the Modern Language Association. The first of these yearly seminars, held in New York in 1968, concentrated on the novelists Theotokas, Myrivilis, and Kazantzakis;

[4] The first fruits of Mrs. Layton's industry appeared in the annual bibliographical supplement of PMLA (*Publications of the Modern Language Association*), June 1969, pp. 1064-73, under the following headings: I. General and Miscellaneous; II. Folklore; III. Medieval Literature in the Vernacular; IV. Literature 1453-1669; V. Literature 1670-1830; VI. Literature 1831-1880; VII. Literature 1881-1922; VIII. Modern Literature after 1922. Each section has subheadings such as General, Poetry, Prose Fiction, Drama and Theatre. Books and periodicals are listed alphabetically according to author under these headings.

[5] The following fields are covered: Archeology, Byzantine and modern Greek history, literature, folklore, art, language, economics, education, the history and dogma of the Greek Orthodox Church, bibliography, and biography.

the second, held in Denver, on the poet Cavafy; and the third, again in New York, on the Greek folksong and its contribution to nineteenth- and twentieth-century literature. The 1971 seminar, held in Chicago, focused on the poetry of Sikelianos.

From the start, however, it was clear that a meeting of one hour and a half each year, even when supplemented by a business meeting, would be hardly enough to satisfy the Association's interest in bringing together, for the sharing of mutual concerns, scholars devoted to all aspects of the field. Especially since another cherished goal, the inauguration of a journal, seemed a relatively long-term project, the executive committee voted to direct the Association's limited initial resources toward a series of biennial symposia lasting three or four days and hopefully offering an opportunity to invite distinguished foreign scholars to meet with their colleagues in this country. The proceedings of the first such symposium, convened at Princeton for three days in the fall of 1969 (October 30 to November 1) and attended by approximately 200 persons, form the basis of this book, to be discussed in detail below. The second symposium, sponsored by the MGSA in cooperation with the Department of Comparative Literature at Harvard and the Fogg Museum, took place in Cambridge on May 7, 8, and 9, 1971, in commemoration of the 150th anniversary of the Greek War of Independence. Because of this historical context, and because the Princeton symposium had focused on literature, the meetings at Harvard were given over chiefly to historical themes, supplemented by papers on the literature most relevant to the occasion and by other cultural manifestations, such as a demonstration of Greek shadow theatre (Karaghiozes).[6] It is hoped that the proceedings of the Harvard symposium will eventually be published in a volume similar to the present one.

In turning now to the Princeton symposium, we should first of all remember that it depended substantially on the administrative assistance provided by the University through its Council of the Humanities and its University Conference office, and also on several generous gifts. The American Council of Learned Societies, anxious to see its new affiliate receive a proper launching, awarded a grant of $5,675. The remainder of symposium expenses (some $2,500) were met by grants from the American Council on the Teaching of Foreign Languages (ACTFL), the Eberhardt Faber Fund, and Mr. Andreas Carnavas. Under

[6] The historical papers included the following: D. Geanakoplos, "The Role of the Greeks of the Diaspora in the Development of the New National Consciousness"; J. Nicolopoulos, "The Greeks of Russia and the Origins of Greek Nationalism"; N. Valaoritis, "Rhigas Pheraios and the Pre-Revolutionary Intellectual Ferment"; G. D. Frangos, "Philike Hetairia and the Greek Revolution"; E. Vlachos, "Social Organization and Social Conflicts at the Time of the Greek War of Independence"; D. Skiotis, "The Greek Revolution: Ali Pasha's Last Gamble"; K. Kazazis, "Some Aspects of Linguistic Hellenocentrism, or Why the Turks Behave Like Turks"; Barbara Jelavich, "The Greek Revolution and the Balkan Nations"; J. Petropulos, "Forms of Collaboration with the Enemy during the Greek War of Independence"; S. Vryonis, "The Greeks under Turkish Rule"; A. Bryer, "The Greeks of the Pontos and the Greek War of Independence"; L. Stavrianos, "Greece in World Historical Perspective"; and H. Psomiades, "The Character of the Modern Greek State." In addition, the symposium offered the following: C. Proussis, "The Memoirs of Makryiannis"; A. Lord, "The Heroic Tradition of Greek Epic and Ballad—Continuity and Change"; and Ann Farmakides, "On Combining the Teaching of Classical and Modern Greek."

this rather munificent budget, the Association was able to invite participants from Athens, Rome, Geneva, and Oxford,[7] in addition to scholars from a wide range of American universities.

Unlike the meetings at Maryland in 1968, the Princeton symposium was unified by a central theme: "Modern Greek Literature and Its European Background." But the planners also included several sessions on the Greek language and modes of teaching it, since these areas of exploration were considered crucially important to the effective and expanded instruction of modern Greek studies in this country.[8] And in addition, the symposium offered

[7] Two of the speakers invited from Greece, Dr. C. Th. Dimaras and Professor George Savidis, were unable to obtain permission to leave Greece in order to participate in the symposium. Dr. Dimaras' paper, included here in the original French version, was read in English translation by Edmund Keeley. Reference to Professor Savidis' work on the new poems of Cavafy was included in the commentary on those poems (see pp. 124ff. below), and the English versions read at the symposium were those he had prepared in collaboration with Edmund Keeley for the Dial Press volume entitled *Passions and Ancient Days*, New York, 1971.

[8] One such session was practical, the other theoretical. During the first, Mrs. Chrysanthi Bien demonstrated a beginning class in modern Greek, using Princeton students as guinea-pigs. She was assisted in this by Professors John Rassias and Peter Bien, who used the occasion to demonstrate their new textbook incorporating the oral/aural/visual techniques developed by Professor Rassias in his work as a director of language instruction for the Peace Corps. The theoretical session involved a panel discussion on university programs in modern Greek. Professor A. Owen Aldridge argued that modern Greek literature could be most conveniently housed in Comparative Literature departments, and he described some courses in this area already offered at Illinois. Dr. Ann Farmakides urged parallel instruction of ancient and modern Greek, citing her own experience in the Department of Classics at McGill. Professor Thanasis Maskaleris stressed "cultural involvement" and indi-

two presentations not directly related to the central theme but regarded as generally relevant. In the first of these Professor C. A. Trypanis surveyed the Greek literary language from classical times to 1800, stressing the recurring efforts in the Roman, Byzantine, and Turkish periods to bring written Greek back to an Attic purity, and then turning to the demotic florescence in Crete under Venetian rule and the subsequent influence this exerted on the schools of Ioannina, Chios, Smyrna, and the Ionian islands. Though only grazing the role of other European

---

cated how he combines modern Greek culture and literature in his courses in the extension division at Berkeley. Mr. Philip Emmanuel called for systematic collaboration between literary men and educators here and in Greece, with the aim of developing viable curricula. Dr. Basil Vlavianos exposed the *bête noire* of *katharevousa*, emphasizing the complications that Greek bilingualism produces in the classroom. Professor Mary Gianos, editor of the Twayne series on modern Greek authors, drew attention to the need for teaching materials, especially translations and criticism, if modern Greek literature is to be offered in our schools as effectively as other contemporary literatures.

Professor John Anton brought the above points together by suggesting that if modern Greek studies are to secure an appropriate place in the curricula of our universities, we must foster and coordinate efforts to produce (1) effective manuals of instruction for the modern Greek language, (2) imaginative courses relating modern Greek literature to other literatures, and (3) a wealth of readily available textbooks, literary texts, and critical commentaries. To put these hopes for the future in perspective, Professor Kostas Kazazis presented the situation as it now exists in America: a plethora of short-lived non-credit courses, an emotional rather than scholarly attitude toward the language, the absence of teacher-training, and uncertainty among instructors regarding the possibilities of offering the language as a major or of even continuing instruction beyond the elementary level. Kazazis argued that we should expand existing programs before attempting to inaugurate new ones.

cultures in this development, the survey offered a helpful general background to the two papers on bilingualism delivered later.

The second presentation not directly related to the symposium's central theme was a reading of, and commentary on, eleven "new" poems by Cavafy. The poems were delivered in Greek by Zissimos Lorenzatos and in English by Edmund Keeley, who read versions he had translated in collaboration with George Savidis. In his commentary, Professor Keeley spoke about the history and relevance of the seventy-five *anekdota* (unpublished) poems that appeared in Athens in 1968, placing these "new" poems in the context of the Cavafy canon as it was then known and describing the particular interest of each new poem selected for reading. His remarks at the symposium became the basis for the essay included in this book.

The remaining papers—twelve in all, of which nine are reproduced here[9]—examined the central theme of the symposium from diverse perspectives. The material they covered ranges in date from the 1820's to the 1960's; includes the three major genres: poetry, prose, and drama; and involves authors resident in mainland Greece, the islands, and the diaspora. Various critical methodologies are in evidence, and Greek literature is scrutinized not only by Hellenes but by barbarians, who presumably see things from a different point of view. A danger invited

[9] The three not included, due to space limitations, focused on writers or themes already represented in the selection offered here: Michael Antonakes on "Reactions (Greek, French, and English) to Kazantzakis' View of the Christ Figure"; M. Byron Raizis on "Kazantzakis' play *Odysseas* and Gerhart Hauptmann's *The Bow of Odysseus*"; and Andreas K. Poulakides on "The Romantic Movement in Greek Literature."

by such diversity is the possible absence of a coherent center despite the shared topic of "Modern Greek Literature and Its European Background." A danger invited by the topic itself is the temptation to enumerate drearily how Greek writer *X* was influenced by European writer *Y*—surely one of the most discouragingly sterile of critical exercises. Readers must judge for themselves whether these dangers have been avoided; in my opinion, they have. Regarding the first: one would have to work extremely hard to make a collection of diverse essays on modern Greek literature *lack* a coherent center. The deeper one goes into this field of study, the more one becomes aware that everything in it relates unavoidably and naturally to everything else, whether or not we strive for coherence. The language itself—that continuous, "mortally immortal" vehicle—is one reason. The self-conscious obsession of all Greeks with their Greekness, even when they are slavishly imitating foreign modes, is another. Further causes of this unavoidable coherence should be evident in the essays that follow and need not be elaborated here. Suffice it to say that in large part the unity felt during the Princeton symposium was *acheiropoietos*: not made by hands.

Regarding the second danger—the dreary enumeration of influences—I believe that the symposium avoided this as well—again, not necessarily owing to skill or forethought, but rather to the nature of the field itself. William Butler Yeats once asserted that great literature arises from a marriage of folk culture and images with individual cultivated urban intelligence. He was speaking primarily of the Irish renaissance, but his formula could be applied equally well to the Chaucerian and Elizabethan florescences in England, the seventeenth-century renaissance in Crete, and other significant instances of concerted artistic excellence. If we think of the great figures involved —Chaucer, Shakespeare, Kornaros, Joyce, Yeats himself— we will note that the "cultivated urban intelligence" residing in each was trained in, and inspired by, foreign modes. Chaucer looked to France, Shakespeare and Kornaros to Italy, Yeats to England and Japan, Joyce to Norway and the Parisian avant garde. Yet each in his own way managed to fuse indigenous folk elements into his sophisticated, borrowed plots, meters, or genres, producing something fresh and remarkable. What I am suggesting, obviously, is that when we examine the European background to modern Greek literature, even if we do this by unimaginatively cataloguing *Y*'s influence upon *X*, we are investigating of necessity the most basic and fascinating problem of all: what caused Greece to blossom.

The essays here suggest again and again that Yeats' formula may be applied to the modern Greek literary renaissance, and they confirm the degree to which the individual intelligences involved were cultivated outside Greece itself, or by foreign influences that had been imported. Solomos, the founder of modern Greek poetry, was Italianate in culture; when he finally discovered his role as a poet writing in Greek, he drew inspiration from Dante, in the ways described so eloquently by Mr. Lorenzatos. Calvos, as Mr. Bouvier tells us, might never have written poetry in Greek if it were not for the currents of European philhellenism he encountered in Geneva. Matesis, like the other Ionian intellectuals of his time, grew up on Italian, French, English, and German literature, yet wedded these influences to the idiomatic and picturesque language of his own time and place, drawing both his characterization and the "problem" of his play from indigenous sources. The Palamas we see in Mr. Maskaleris' essay was so busy reading Goethe, Hugo, Leconte de Lisle, Prudhomme, *les symbolistes*, Mistral, Verhaeren, Tolstoy, Ibsen, Nietzsche, D'Annunzio, Pascoli, Unamuno, Hardy, and William James, that it is a wonder he found time to write anything of his own. Yet he not only wrote voluminously; he assimilated all the foreign influences, married them to indigenous reality and dream, and produced an *oeuvre* that was both individual and national. His urban intelligence was cultivated largely outside his own land and time (though physically he never left Greece), but his hero was the gypsy—the "mortally immortal" ever-wandering Greek.

If we consider Kazantzakis, we see essentially the same dichotomies, though we are not so sure of the happy conclusion. Brought up under the great shadow of Palamas' eclecticism (everything in modern Greek literature relates to everything else!), Kazantzakis—possibly because he was physically removed from his land for extended periods—had much more difficulty in disciplining this eclecticism so that it might speak to the specific condition of his people. He clung to the demotic language championed by Solomos, Matesis, and Palamas, but this was not enough: his truly significant work came only when he was willing to honor other aspects of the folk culture and to allow himself to see the world through at least one eye that was native and unsophisticated.

Finally, coming to Seferis, we are presented in Peter Levi's study with "a poet who became possible only because of the central tradition of European poetry in the late nineteenth century," yet one whose cultivated urban intelligence took the influences "available" to him—those of Rimbaud, Eliot, and Laforgue, for example—and squeezed them into the cap of a mortally immortal Greek sailor, his most characteristic protagonist.

But all formulas about literature, including the one by Yeats that I have been applying, are extremely dangerous if we do not qualify, or perhaps even abandon, them after they have rendered service. These essays would indeed be formulaic in the worst sense if they showed Greek writers doing nothing more than turning outward toward western European models in order to gain sophistication, or if they implied that there have been no changes or developments during the century and a half we are considering. Fortunately, the essays collected here do not fall into either of these traps.

Mr. Maskaleris, after cataloguing Palamas' European sources, quite rightly reminds us that ancient and Byzantine writings were also vitally active in the cultivated intelligence that this author wedded to folk culture. As we all know, Greek writers turned not only outward to Europe, but backward to their own past. What the essays here help us to realize, however, is that the division is misleading. Calvos' hellenism was inspired by his contacts with western Europe. The cult of the ancients injected into Greek education and linguistic consciousness by Solomos' bogyman Koraes was a Europeanized one, the result of Koraes' admiration for the western Renaissance and Enlightenment. In short, though the Greeks looked backward as well as outward, they tended at first to see their history through western European eyes, slighting the Byzantine years in favor of an idealized, distorted conception of the Golden Age. But even when (here, Mr. Dimaras' essay is very suggestive) the inevitable reaction took place and Paparrigopoulos' monumental history established Byzantium as the crucial link joining ancient and modern Greece, and established as well the dogma that the history of the Greek people is single, unified, and continuous, this was once more a looking backward through the lenses of European consciousness, in this instance through the Romanticism that was then everywhere in the ascendant.

What we see, therefore, are cultivated urban intelligences whose sophistication involves a contemporaneity (outward looking) and historicity (backward looking) that are mixed very closely together. The situation becomes even more complicated when we realize—as Mr. Dimaras wisely says we must—that this hybrid was then wedded to "indigenous" elements by no means entirely distinguishable from it, for the vogue of folk language and culture, something we might have considered impeccably native, was itself shaped by Western European Romanticism.

Yeats' formula seems to have degenerated into a target yearning to be riddled with qualifications, and yet we all know instinctively, without need of fancy proof, that modern Greek literature arose from a merger of the foreign with the indigenous, the cultivated with the popular. It is at this point that we must cease viewing the hundred and fifty years between Solomos and Seferis as though they were static. I said earlier that the essays in the present volume do not fall into this trap; on the contrary, if we view them synoptically, they suggest very interesting lines of development. They suggest, first of all, that Greek writers, though perhaps initially prodded to look outward, backward, and even inward because of their *xenomania*, gradually learned to see all these aspects of reality through their own, not borrowed, eyes—to see them through their ears as well, one might venture, since the way the poet or novelist hears the contemporaneity and historicity around him, the way he makes us hear it, in short the language he employs, is such a crucial factor in Greek individuality.

The most startling example is Cavafy. Completely conversant with poetic fashion in Europe, he nevertheless approached the Greek past and present in a wholly individualistic way, exploiting the Paparrigopoulian dogma of a continuous, mortally-immortal Greece in a manner inconceivable in a Western writer. As Edmund Keeley suggests, Cavafy's successful struggle to achieve a forthright and unpretentious, if sometimes highly dramatic, language, as he explored the meaning of Hellenism in both himself and his tradition, served more than anything to establish him as the most original Greek poet of this century, whether one listens to his voice in the collected poems or in the newly published poems introduced here. The originality is first of all a matter of what Peter Levi calls "tone of voice": the unique signature that expresses and guarantees a writer's individuality. Using as his example Seferis—a poet, we remember, "who became possible only because of the central traditions of European poetry in the late nineteenth century"—Peter Levi stresses how inseparable this tone is from language, how by Seferis' time the Greek tongue had come to carry its own moral and aesthetic values, enabling the poet to exploit it as a context, with nonchalance and assurance.

If we view our essays synoptically, however, we are

reminded that the nonchalant genuineness one senses in Seferis was an achievement won only after long struggle. In the realm of their own language as well as in everything else, cultivated Greeks had to purge themselves gradually of European eyes and ears; only when they had done so were they content to allow this indigenous element to exist unmolested. The essays show the Europeanized vision of classicizers and demoticists alike. The latter, because they were polemicists, could not be nonchalant. They had to prove something, had to mold the language instead of allowing themselves to be molded by it. Kazantzakis is a particularly interesting, and tragic, example, embroiled as he was in the crusade begun so innocently by Solomos, manipulating the language (though with the best of intentions), and compromising his own artistry because he saw himself as a crusader in the European tradition and because he subscribed indiscriminately to a romantic view of the "folk." But perhaps the Kazantzakian embroilment is a pre-condition of the Cavafian or Seferian assurance. Perhaps someone has to choke on certain ingredients before someone else can swallow them.

Viewed synoptically, the essays suggest this development. They also show how Greece, like Western Europe, began with a literature almost exclusively poetic and then introduced the novel at a later stage. There are six essays on poets, only one on prose, an imbalance that bears tacit witness to certain assumptions still very much alive. Once again, Kazantzakis becomes an interesting example, this time of a man with a greater natural talent for prose than for verse, yet tragically denying this talent because prose was considered an inferior medium. Prose is now becoming firmly established in Greece; Mr. Vitti's essay shows some of its growing pains, and how, over a span of several generations, it has attempted to treat the fashionable European concern of alienation in an individual way, providing us, incidentally, with another instance where Yeats' insight may be applied profitably to Greek letters. The increasing acceptance of prose has naturally affected poetry and will continue to do so. How each genre modifies the other, and how, separately and concertedly, they continue to assimilate foreign influences, wedding these to things indigenous, will undoubtedly occupy future scholars.

I have tried to show certain elements of overt and covert unity in these diverse essays on the European background of modern Greek literature, and I have also tried to show why this general topic brings us willynilly to the most fundamental problem of all: what made Greece suddenly blossom forth artistically. Each reader will also ask this question personally and will keep looking for those special qualities which somehow constitute the "Greekness" of the literary renaissance we are considering. Is it primarily the language that gives this literature its signature? Or the awareness of survival, interruption, and continuity? Or the sense of loss infused with hope? Or the plasticity, the immersion in the palpable immediacy of Greece's landscape? Or the ability to look outward, backward, and inward at the same time? Or all of these, and more?

It would be wrong to expect definitive answers to such questions. Yet a collection of essays should at least pose the problems and grope toward some solution. The Modern Greek Studies Association trusts that this book will be a beginning in this process, and, if nothing else, that it will help to awaken English-speaking readers and educators to the creative wealth of modern Greece, a wealth that has been so unjustifiably neglected until now in our schools and in our humanistic studies at all levels.

PETER BIEN

Woodbrooke
Birmingham, England
February, 1971

Zissimos Lorenzatos

1. *Solomos'*

DIALOGOS:

A Survey

To J.G.

after so many years

ALL countries have their own distinctive standards. But in spite of this, one may draw certain parallels, and occasionally these parallels have some foundation. It seems to me that a parallel with some foundation can be drawn between the two ancient classical languages, Greek and Latin. I am not referring to these languages as they were in antiquity—that would have no connection with the purpose of this essay—but to the fate they have known with the passage of time in the respective areas where they used to be spoken and written or where they have ceased to be spoken and written: the Greek language, with its continuous development, in modern Greece, and the Latin language, with its final demise, in medieval Italy. The *Dialogos* of Solomos, which concerns modern Greek literature, and the *De Vulgari Eloquentia* of Dante, which concerns the European or Western tradition, are two parallel texts that are directly related to the two parallel languages and to the path these languages took successively in Dante's time in Italy and in Solomos' time in Greece.

Both texts have come down to us in a fragmentary state: that of Dante because it was never finished, and that of Solomos because the complete work has never been found (though there is no reason why the missing part should not be found one day). We know that Solomos finished the *Dialogos*, because in July or August of 1825 he asked a friend of his, L. Stranis, whether he would like the work to be dedicated to him: "Desidero di sapere se ti fo cosa grata a dedicarti il *Dialogo*." Dante's text, *il trattatello*, as it has always been called by the Italians, was written in Latin in order to attack Latin and to plead the cause of the national language of the Italians, which at that time was called *il volgare*, the vulgar language, from the Latin *lingua vulgaris.* The text of Solomos was written in the national language of Greece in order to demonstrate, with Solomos' own writing as the model, that the written language of every nation not only must be, but can be, what it must be: the written expression of the spoken, or mother tongue, and nothing else.

The *De Vulgari Eloquentia* was published two centuries after Dante's death, first anonymously in the Italian translation of Trissino (Vicenza, 1529), and later in the Latin original (Paris, 1577) edited by a certain Corbinelli, a Florentine exile. In the beginning the translation was not considered genuine, as was also the case with Solomos' *Dialogos,* and approximately half a century elapsed before the Dantean original was published. Solomos himself read the translation of Trissino, as we know from an early notebook which has been photocopied and typographically reproduced in the monumental two-volume edition of Solomos' *Manuscripts* published in Thessaloniki in 1964 (*Αὐτόγραφα Ἔργα,* ed. L. Politis).

In drawing our parallel between Dante and Solomos, it is essential at the outset to remember that the one belonged to the faith of the Western Church and the other to that of the Eastern Church. Both are poets with religious or metaphysical roots. Unless we take this into account, we shall misunderstand both of them. At the very time when the contemporaries of Solomos were "shedding their blood beneath the Cross," he was fighting to serve the living spoken language with the help of the Word from Heaven, exactly as Dante notes at the beginning of his essay: "Verbo aspirante de coelis, locutioni vulgarium gentium prodesse tentabimus." *Prodesse* means to aid the language. Dante did in fact aid the national language of the Italian people: the language of the common man, *vulgarium gentium*. And that same friend of Solomos mentioned previously, L. Stranis, wrote with foresight from Zante on January 15, 1822, that the poet was devoting all his energy to the formation of the modern Greek language: "... E pone ogni sua cura nel formare la Lingua Greca moderna" (*Rime Improvisate*, 1822). Dante had said in his *Convivio* that he would speak more fully about the common language in a book that, with the help of God, he was preparing: "Di questo si parlerà altrove più compiutamente in un libro ch'io intendo di fare, Dio concedente, di *volgare eloquenzia*" (I. 5). In a similar manner Solomos covertly declares in the *Dialogos* that "a book will shortly be published, written in the language of the people of Greece. . . . They told me that the author is a young man [Solomos wrote the *Dialogos* when he was about 25 years old] who is always fighting for the common language."

Let us start with the *De Vulgari Eloquentia*. There exists, according to Dante, both the "vulgaris locutio" and the "grammatica locutio," as the Romans called it. That "secundariam locutionem," the secondary language, the Greeks also have: "Graeci habent." We may add here that in Byzantium the 12th-century poems attributed to Theodoros Prodromos call the archaic written language of the Byzantines "ta grammatika"—Dante's *grammatica*—a language learned with "great difficulty": "*Καὶ ἔμαθον τὰ γραμματικὰ μετὰ πολλοῦ τοῦ κόπου.*" There is, then, the language, this *locutio*, that we learn without difficulty: "sine omni regula"; and that which we learn with great effort only: "per spatium temporis et studii assiduitatem," or as stated in the words of Prodromos: "*μετὰ πολλοῦ τοῦ κόπου.*" We learn without effort as we imitate our nurse, "nutricem immitantes," and this is our first true language: "nostra vera prima locutio." This national speech of every country, or the living tongue, is not only *not* vulgar, but it is more noble than the other ("nobilior est vulgaris") for two fundamental reasons: because man uses it first: "tum quia prima fuit humano generi usitata," and because everyone speaks it: "tum quia totus orbis ipsa perfruitur." One language is natural or true for us: "naturalis est nobis," the other artificial or unnatural: "potius artificialis." And for Dante, Latin is such an artificial or unnatural language. It was a daring thing to say for that time, when all serious works were written in Latin, which was the language not only of the great literary tradition and of Virgil (whom Dante addresses as "great river of speech": di parlar sì largo fiume" [*Inf.* 1. 80]), but also of the Church. A daring thing to say also because that century of the exiled Dante, as most centuries of mankind, was a savage century: "secol selvaggio" (*Purg.* 16. 135). Later, after the death of the poet of the *Divine Comedy*, it was still not certain for many years in Italy whether it would be lawful and proper to write serious works in the common language. And Petrarch thought that his fame would depend far more on his Latin works (virtually unread today) than on his *Canzionere*, written in Italian.

A common language grows out of dialects and is itself a complementary dialect needed for common understanding: a logical or mathematical product of the dialects standing alongside the other dialects, the crowning proof of the linguistic and spiritual unity of every people. Dante hunts throughout the woods and pastures of Italy ("saltus et pascua Italiae") to seize that panther ("pantheram") which, as he tells us, one can smell everywhere but which is nowhere to be found: "redolentem ubique et necubi apparentem." Further on he seeks to find, in an Aristotelian or more logical manner ("rationabilius"), some standard or type ("signum") against which to gauge the common speech, as we gauge numbers against the unit, colors against white, deeds against virtue, and, lastly, all the characteristics constituting the "Italianness" of the Italians that cannot be found in particular in any city but which are common to all: "nullius civitatis Italiae propria sunt et in omnibus communia sunt."

One of these characteristics Dante considers to be the living language through which all communicate beyond or outside the local coloring of their particular language and whose scent is to be found in all regions without being found in any particular region: "illud . . . vulgare . . . quod in qualibet redolet civitate, nec cubat in ulla," in other words, the voice present in every town without seeming to belong to any particular town: "quod omnis . . . civitatis est et nullius esse videtur" (I. 16). This same "vulgare" occurs commonly in all parts of the nation without being particular to any one region: "omnibus . . . commune nec proprium ulli" (I. 18). The Italian translation of Trissino, which, as we have noted, was known to Solomos, reads: "commune a tuti, e proprio di niuno." Here we have the origin of Solomos' well-known maxim, "il commune e proprio": "the common and the essential" (*τὸ κοινὸ καὶ τὸ κύριο*, according to the established translation of Polylas). This maxim may have been understood at a later time in a general or abstract sense, thus assuming unforeseeable philosophical proportions, but originally

Solomos thought of it not abstractly or philosophically, but in direct relation to the language: "radicato ed immedesimato colla lingua"—"rooted in and identified with the language," again as Polylas translates it. In both the *De Vulgari Eloquentia* and in the "Thoughts" of Solomos' Ἐλεύθεροι Πολιορκημένοι (*The Free Besieged*), the phrase about the common and the particular refers first of all to the language: this is its point of departure. And only by starting with the language can one subsequently apply it elsewhere. It is on this basis that Solomos names that which belongs to all ("commune") and that which belongs to the individual ("proprio"), that which is common to everyone and particular to everyone. I cite the whole sentence from the established text of the first publisher: "Il tuono fondamentale del poema sia dal principio alla fine il commune e proprio radicato et immedesimato colla lingua." ("Let the fundamental rhythm of the poem be from start to finish the common and the essential, rooted in and identified with the language.")

Dante was the founder of the language of Italian literature as Solomos was the founder of the language of modern Greek literature. But we may observe an important difference between the two countries. Whereas in Italy the unification of the language (primarily through Dante) occurred some five hundred years earlier than the political unification, in Greece the political and linguistic unification (with Solomos) took place simultaneously; it is another matter if in Greece a different solution was arbitrarily imposed (a matter that we shall consider below). In this respect Greece differs from other countries where the political preceded the linguistic unification, as in England and France, and from countries where the political disunity continued for centuries after the linguistic unification, as in Germany, the language having been established by Luther (1483-1546) with his model translation of the Bible, three hundred years before the political unification. Of course those who establish a tradition do not emerge "out of nothing." In Dante's Italy, as in the Greece of Solomos, we find models and grammars, and there were men and women who did listen to or speak the language identified with the vision of each people and with the history of its soul. The first grammarian of the Italian "volgare," Guido Faba of Bologna, paved the way in theoretical terms for Dante's *De Vulgari Eloquentia.*

The notion that the Italian language began with Dante by no means signifies that the Latin language ended with him. As we know, Latin was still used for centuries (and not only in Italy) by the state, and in education, science, law, and diplomacy. In fact, Latin was not abolished in France as a legal language until 1539, when it was finally superseded by French. In Hungary the various draft laws were debated in Latin as late as 1840, and in Poland even later. This is another matter. What is indisputable, however, is that over Greece and Italy hung directly—not indirectly as in other lands—the shadow of the two classical languages, and that in Italy the so-called "questione della lingua" and the language problem in Greece are specifically related to the pressure exercised successively by the two great classical traditions.

So Dante discovered all the various dialects in his country, but next to the dialects he searched for the common language of the whole of Italy: "Et sicut omnia hic est invenire, sic et illud quod totius Italiae est" (I. 19). One should take up this language and elevate it with mastery and force: "magistratu et potestate." And this is to be done by those who are most capable. Then the language elevates its own creators, or it raises them up with honor and glory: "Et vulgare de quo loquimur, et sublimatum est magistratu et potestate, et suos honore sublimat et gloria." Among so many crude words ("rudibus vocabulis") one needs to untangle confusing constructions ("perplexis constructionibus"), defective pronunciations ("defectivis prolationibus"), rustic accents ("rusticanis accentibus"), and thus to make the common language a distinguished medium ("egregium"), clear ("extricatum"), complete ("perfectum"), and highly polished or urbane ("et urbanum") (1. 17). Once one has struggled to make this common language a suitable and ready medium for every need, then the great poets appear, the model ones: "magni poetae, hoc est regulares"—either in poetry or in prose—those who write ("poetati sunt") maintaining the rules of the craft ("arte regulari") and not like others who write casually ("casu"), more by chance than by craft ("casu magis quam arte") (2. 4). These finally elevate languages and ennoble poetic forms, opening the latch on the workshop of art ("artis ergasterium reseremus").

Now the *Dialogos* of Solomos.

That Solomos shared the idea that one must first submit to his national language in order to dominate it later, is made clear in the *Dialogos*, where the words Bacon applied to the philosopher and nature—"naturae non imperatur nisi parendo"—are applied to the writer and language: "first submit to the language of the people, and then if you are able, master it." Language can be likened, one might say, to a horse or a ship; it carries you, but you hold the reins or the rudder. Here are the Dantean rules of Solomos: ". . . the writer sometimes follows the people in his phrasing, and sometimes not; the form of the words employed by the people is not changed by the writer; to be ennobled each word needs but the skill of the writer." It is also made clear in the letter, written in Italian, which Solomos sent to G. Tertsetis from Zakynthos on June 1, 1833; here Solomos speaks of using the language of the demotic songs as a "starting point" only, not of stopping there: "Whoever makes use of the klephtic language ought to use it in its essence, not merely formally—do you understand what I'm saying?" ("Chi si usa della lingua clefta lo facesse virtualmente, non formalmente, m'intendi?") "And as for poetry . . . it is certainly good to tread in those tracks, but not to stop there: one must raise oneself up perpendicularly" ("E quanto al poetare . . . e bene si, piantarsi su quelle orme, ma non e bene fermarvisi: conviene alzarsi perpendicolarmente"). The poetry of the Klephts, an unaffected manifestation ("ingenuo manifestazione") of a certain vision or way of life, "does not have the same meaning when *we* speak it: the nation seeks from us the treasure of our individual intelligence clad in a national dress." ("Non ha l'istesso interesse in bocca nostra: la nazione vuole da noi il tesoro della nostra intelligenza individuale vestito nazionalmente.") The national dress is, of course, the national language.

I mention the letter of Solomos to G. Tertsetis here because it is, after the *Dialogos*, the second most important text concerning language that we possess by Solomos. Written about ten years later, it refers at one point, if I am not mistaken, to the then unpublished *Dialogos*, which the friends of Solomos would have known. (Among these is the recipient of the letter, who saved the important *Dialogos* itself for us.) The point I have in mind is the following. In his *Dialogos*, Solomos, taking advantage of the controversy about the written language and the use of Latin in France, Germany, and Italy, emphasizes that "the most learned men of those nations wanted to write a language which had at one time lived on the lips of men [that is to say, Latin], but our own learned men want us to write a language that is neither spoken now, nor has ever been spoken in any other period, nor shall ever be spoken in the future." He was here speaking of the "*katharevousa*," which, in keeping with the Dantean terminology that we saw earlier, might better have been called "δευτερεύουσα"—"secundaria locutio." It is to this *katharevousa*—whose power of being a serious obstacle to the progressive formation of a written language (i.e., the written expression of the oral language) he had underestimated when young—that Solomos refers in his letter to Tertsetis; and he accuses himself of lacking discernment: "With how little discernment did I set myself to ridicule this language of Babel before our own had made any progress." ("Della poca prudenza con cui mi posi a deridere quella lingua Babelica, prima che questa nostra facesse progressi.")

Progress in the written language in Greece since those days has been retarded dangerously, and only with indefatigable discipline in our writing can we now perhaps not replace, but at least somehow reduce, the time lost. "But my soul aches," Solomos declares again and again—four times—in the handwritten fragments of his *Dialogos* as he sees that there are people living in his own age "who try to deprive" the fighters of 1821 "of their language"—"my soul aches." Solomos' pain is always with us.

In the *Dialogos* we also encounter the Dantean concepts concerning the common language and the dialects, along with the systematic search for the panther of the common language ("pantheram quam sequimur"), the language in which we Greeks "understand one another" whether we come "from Mani," or "from Gastouni . . . Mt. Olympos . . . Chios . . . Philippoupolis . . . Missolonghi . . . Constantinople." And just as we have our customs and manners (in the words of Dante, "simplicissima signa et morum et habituum"), to serve as "weights and measures" for our actions as Greeks (what Dante, speaking of the Italians, calls "quibus latine actiones ponderantur et mensurantur"), so we possess a Greek language in which we "understand one another" as Greeks. Both we find not in any one city of Greece (or of Italy), but in all cities in common ("Haec nullius civitatis Italiae propria sunt," concludes Dante, "et in omnibus communia sunt") (I. 16).

These and other parallels that can be drawn between the *Dialogos* and the *De Vulgari Eloquentia* do not reveal a shallow influence or imitation. The influence of Dante on the works of Solomos penetrates so deeply that it is not necessary for us to look for external evidence. It is a self-evident truth. With these remarks we but continue our original comparison between the fates of the two ancient languages, Latin and Greek, in Dante's Italy and Solomos' Greece. And on the basis of the two related texts we shall attempt a survey—mainly of Solomos' *Dialogos* and of Greece's controversial language problem. It is in countries such as Greece, with long-established precedents, that the most insignificant question requires an investigation often covering unlimited periods of time. Greece is a country with a heritage that stretches very far back in history. Perhaps that is the counterpoise for having become a small country. But in any case we would have to spread out our maps of the last two thousand years in order to comprehend completely the significance that the *Dialogos* of Solomos holds for us, a significance related to Dante's message in his *De Vulgari Eloquentia.*

Three times in the past two thousand years, with various lesser movements in between, the learned tradition (that is, the tradition that maintains that the language we write must not be the written expression of the spoken language, but some *other* language) has attempted to dominate the written word, promising people that the observing of its canon would mark the beginning of the creation of great works. In these two thousand years it seems there has not been enough time for people to realize that the promise was a lie or that the canon was not valid. Not a single great work has been created, nor has "the glory of our ancestors" been resurrected, with the dual case and the optative mood. We have wasted untold energy in order to distort our nature and to smother our soul and our speech with the makeup of rhetoric. Since the period of antiquity the learned tradition has never left the natural development of the written language unhampered; and every time the natural language has begun to emerge from obscurity, dressed in all the colors of life, the learned tradition has pushed it back or has hidden it away in its permanently neglected corner. For two thousand years we have watched the story of beautiful Cinderella and her stepmother being played with the Greek language. I am not among those who suffer the misfortune of observing everything with "objective" eyes. God has protected me from being condemned to such a sentence. But I do not want to let emotion carry me away and to become angry. I believe that only God's anger is just; man's is not. Man's voice is justified only when it has a human warmth and when "it seeketh not its own." The voices of Solomos and Dante have proved to be such voices.

The first time that the learned tradition unsheathed itself was with the Atticism of the 1st century B.C., which was inaugurated in Rome through the initiative of Dionysius of Halicarnassus ("von dem bornierten [narrow-minded] Rhetor Dionysios von Halikarnass," as Krumbacher calls him),[1] whose influence was sustained through the first four centuries of the Christian era and beyond. Subsequently, from A.D. 330 on, when Constantinople became the capital of the Roman Empire and Christianity the state religion, the Church—which throughout the initial period of the martyrs and apologists had used the simple language (one could even say that the New Testament is the most ancient monument of the modern language)—was forced to accept the language of Greek education, and during the 4th century A.D., the Fathers of the Church also "atticized" their language. Basil the Great, in writing to Libanius concerning the sacred texts, says that they have "νοῦν μὲν ἀληθῆ, λέξιν δὲ ἀμαθῆ" ("a true mind but an uneducated idiom"; Migne 32. 1084). In the Western Church there was no need for a linguistic change within the same language. There the Church had passed directly from Greek—which it used up to the mid-

[1] *Das Problem der neugriechischen Schriftsprache*, Munich, 1902, p. 20.

dle of the 3rd century A.D.—to an entirely different language. From then on Latin was the spoken medium. Atticism, on the other hand, had immeasurably obstructive consequences, not for the spoken aspect of the living language—no one can stop life—but for the written aspect: it prevented the written development of the living speech of the period, that which has been called *κοινὴ* and which we see written on the papyri and in the Gospels. Atticism crippled the written workmanship or craft of this language.

The second time the learned tradition asserted itself was during what has been called the "humanistic renaissance" of the Komnenoi and Paleologoi, from the 11th to the 15th centuries. This simultaneously checked two trends: (a) the attempt made by a few from the 6th to the 10th century to write—or at least to approach when writing—the common spoken language, which was no longer the Hellenistic or Alexandrian *κοινή*, but the language of the medieval period: that which was spoken in the Byzantine Empire (among those who made the attempt were Malalas in the 6th century, Leontios in the 7th century, Theophanes in the 8th century, and Constantine Porphyrogennitos in the 10th century); and (b) the similar attempt made by a few during the humanistic renaissance, e.g., the 12th-century poems of Prodromos, the Acritan epics and the 13th-century Χρονικὸν τοῦ Μορέως (*Chronicle of Morea*).

As we learn from the *Vita Nuova*, Dante himself was aware of the fact that in Byzantium, "in Grecia," people were continuing the practice of writing not the common or simple but the learned language ("non volgari ma litterati poeti"), which was just the opposite of the situation in Provence ("lingua d' *Oco*") and in Italy ("lingua di *Sì*"), where for nearly one hundred and fifty years—that is, from about 1150—love poetry had been written in the simple language ("dicitori d'Amore in lingua volgare," xxv). Parallel with these two movements of the learned tradition are three attempts to write in the spoken language: the New Testament, the Byzantine prose writings of the 6th to the 10th or 11th centuries, and the many simply written texts that begin to appear after the 12th century. Three times Cinderella had to bow her head and retreat to her corner, with neither of the traditions finally prevailing. Between those two periodical movements—the one involving the written expression of our voice and the other involving the silencing of it—our spiritual life or our spiritual death have every so often been thrown into the balance: a strange fate.

The third time that the learned tradition showed itself was in the 19th century, at the very moment when we were beginning to form our common written language. This was no longer either the κοινή or the medieval language, but modern Greek, which we conventionally mark off from the medieval language with the fall of Constantinople in 1453, but which had already been almost fully formed in the poems of Prodromos and the *Chronicle of Morea* in the 12th and 13th centuries. The grammar of this language has remained that which was spoken by the people from at least the 15th to the 19th centuries, possibly from much earlier, with only a few changes. I said above "the moment when we were beginning to form our written language," but I said so bearing in mind its brilliant manifestations in the 16th and 17th centuries, especially in Crete, and again in the Ionian Islands in the early 19th century. This was the critical time of Solomos. Alongside the living speech, shaped during the centuries by following its natural development, was the phenomenon of the written language, which continued to use the pre-Christian grammar, obstinately clung to the rules of Atticism, and which had become, we might say, even more archaic in the late centuries, for instance during the humanistic renaissance of the Komnenoi and Paleologoi that I mentioned earlier. Anna Komnena (11th century), Psellos (also 11th century), and Michael Akominatos (12th century), together with countless others, would be used as linguistic models by most of the learned men of the period of enslavement under the Turks.

When Adamantios Koraes (1748-1833) saw this situation, he understood the obvious slackness of Atticism, and he was the first to realize the importance that the study of the modern Greek language could assume. But for Koraes this importance was philological or linguistic; as well as helping the philologist to understand or annotate the ancient language, the study of modern Greek could be used for "correcting" the common language. One might say that the philological and linguistic glory of Koraes was the parallel he drew between the ancient and the modern languages. In working out this parallel he used the example of Eustathios of Thessaloniki (12th century), though we do not know whether Eustathios regarded this parallel as truly useful or whether he drew it out of curiosity because, as Koraes says, "he did it rarely, and he received little help from it in elucidating the Poet [meaning Homer], and almost none in correcting the common language, whose barbarism increased more and more." Koraes goes on to say: "By correcting the language I mean not only transforming various barbarisms in diction and syntax, but also preserving many other words which those who have not studied the language carefully are trying to ban as barbarisms."[2]

The limited credit that Koraes earns from having defamed Atticism or "the impropriety of the Hellenizers" during his time must be offset by his complete inability to understand what was hidden behind the various attempts by people, in both the East and the West, to put their natural voice down on paper, justifiably setting aside the two silenced classical languages, whether in poetry or prose. Koraes disdained or neglected the importance of the various models that were the basis of Dante's linguistic effort, as well as the comparable effort by Solomos. With reference to the West, he mentions "the barbarous writings published there during the 10th century and later, in both prose and verse." And with reference to the East he writes: ". . . Various barbarous writings saw the light; they are worthy of being buried in the earth forever." One of his sentences about the *Erotokritos*, in another letter to his friend A. Vassiliou (Feb. 2, 1805), will remain a classic, condemning this wise man forever: "I confess that it is not a seemly occupation for a person to read the *Erotokritos* and other such freakish offspring of poor tormented Greece." This masterpiece of modern Greek expression, which embodies the psychic rhythm of the whole world of 17th-century Crete in its 15-syllable verse, was called "freakish" by Koraes. He often mouthed the disreputable epithet "vulgar," or "vulgaris" of the learned tradition, when talking about the common language or its products,

[2] Letter to A. Vassiliou—Prologue to *Heliodorus' Aethiopica*, Paris, 1804, 2 vols. (Ἡλιοδώρου Αἰθιοπικά).

and in an undated letter to D. Proios, he laughingly called Vincenzo Kornaros, that great poetic force who wrote the *Erotokritos*, "the Homer of crude literature up to the present time."

In view of this attitude by a Greek whose good faith cannot be questioned, one does not know what to say about the strangeness of human nature and about the ill fate of Greece when one considers Fauriel's courageous introduction to the "Klephtic printed songs," which was written at that same time and which Solomos refers to in the *Dialogos*.[3] In this introduction (p. 124) Fauriel hymns our national language when, in giving advice to Greek writers, he prophesies that "modern Greek will soon be a language which, without resembling ancient Greek more than it now resembles it, will have no reason to envy it."

We have many such examples of appreciation by Koraes' contemporaries, both Greek and foreign. It is not the fault of the times but of the man: Koraes was not a thinker. He tried submissively to transfer Western enlightenment to Greece during his century by adapting it to local conditions or—worse still—by adapting local conditions to Western enlightenment, with the same submissiveness of those who tried to transfer the philosophical and politico-economic system of Marx-Engels to Greece in the 20th century. The analogy brings into conjunction two foreign movements responsible for a fundamental disturbance—one might say psychosis—in Greece, because they are both movements irreconcilable with Greek life. But this is not the occasion to make generalizations. The

[3] C. Fauriel, *Chants populaires de la Grèce moderne*, Vol. I, Paris, 1824; Vol. II, Paris, 1825.

only thing of interest to us here is Koraes' particular failing.

A pupil of Voltaire and an admirer of Gibbon, Koraes had no respect for Byzantium, nor did he understand in depth the spiritual values of the Orthodox Church and of Byzantine civilization. His prejudice against monasticism is well known; he never lost an opportunity to express his anger against it or to slander monks.[4] The spiritual culture that was preserved in the enslaved nation and on which the nation must depend in order to progress, Koraes did not see, nor did he suspect its existence. Everything lay there, submerged "in the miserable centuries of barbarism," asleep "in the deep slumber of ignorance." He expected the rebirth of the nation to come from the classics, and he mobilized all his wisdom and his tireless in-

[4] After reading in the French newspaper *Moniteur* (Feb. 25, 1803) about the twenty-four dialogues of Plato that D. E. Clarke "brought back" (a rapportés) from Patmos, Koraes noted: ". . . And yet these two sources of learning [Patmos and Athos] have denuded all of Greece of its precious manuscripts and have betrayed to a foreign nation, maybe for a little silver, our ancestral inheritance" (Ἰσοκράτους Λόγοι καὶ Ἐπιστολαί [*Speeches and Letters of Isocrates*], Athens, 1807). Actually, in 1801 D. E. Clarke seized Plato's Codex by force from the hands of the monks, with the help of mercenaries and with the acquiescence of the Turks (see I. Sakellion, Πατμιακὴ Βιβλιοθήκη [*Patmian Library*], 1890, p. 1, fn. 5; the Codex is now called Clarcianus 39 and is held in Oxford). S. Kougeas makes the following observation on this subject: "Some admirers of this precious monument, instead of expressing their gratitude towards the monks of Patmos for having preserved it intact during whole centuries, paradoxically spoke about them with scorn and contempt. Equally unjust was Koraes' fury against the monks of Patmos" (Ὁ Καισαρείας Ἀρέθας καὶ τὸ ἔργον αὐτοῦ [*Arethas of Caesaria and His Work*], 1913, p. 99, fn. 4).

dustry for the editing of ancient writers, so that the barbarized Greeks might hold once again the golden thread of the classical, hellenistic, and Roman periods that was cut for a thousand years and more by an impenetrable darkness: Byzantium. Koraes had in mind either the fate "of the common language, whose barbarism increased more and more," or "the fourth, fifth, and following centuries, during which the vulgarity of the Greek race grew." This golden thread, which various renaissance movements in Greek letters maintained or witnessed during the thousand dark years, had been rediscovered in the West by the Renaissance, and this was what they, the Greeks, had to get hold of again in the East, even belatedly, in order to achieve their own eventual renaissance and become naturalized as an "enlightened nation" of Europe.

Koraes systematized Western enlightenment (with its classical ideals) for his fellow countrymen, and became its nucleus for them. The whole learned tradition found a patriarch in his person—whether he wanted it or not—and cried out in one voice the awkward words: *Habemus papam*, "We have a Pope!" We must not fool ourselves on this point. If the learned tradition is a "hodgepodge" like the "*Σύροι, Γραικοί, Ἀρμένιοι, Μῆδοι*" of Cavafy's Mesopotamian Osroene, so too is Koraes—that is to say, he belongs to the hodgepodge of the learned tradition. This hodgepodge could take on various shades, from Koraes' *middle way* to the archaizing mandarins of Atticism—Kommetas, Doukas, Kodrikas—or even to the philhellenic enthusiasm of some strange people like the American Dr. A. Rose, who assured us that "the Greek of today is essentially old Attic Greek," in a lecture before the German Medical Society of New York on February 3, 1896.[5]

But all these shades, which conflict or clash with each other to no end, belong to the learned tradition, and all evade that single proper rule that decrees that the written language must be the written expression of the spoken or mother tongue. From that point of view, it seems almost a minor detail today that Koraes was against the "extreme purists" or even the "half-hellenizing or the half-barbarizing" (Μιξελλενίζοντας ἢ μιξοβαρβάρους). Though he categorically denounced the "bad and perverse habit, still prevailing, of scorning the modern language," did he ever present a linguistically firmer alternative or did he work with the "common language" as a base, as he taught in contradiction to his own practice? And yet this same man realized, and set down in writing, that "we have a great need to write in the language we understand"; and he also realized, and set down in writing, that in the West "they truly started freeing themselves from barbarism when their few learned men first began writing in their common language." A mystery. We could say about Koraes what he says about the modern Greek public, or the "vulgar ones," using Aristophanes' words about the Athenian public in the *Knights* (42): "a difficult and deaf old man," meaning he himself was a difficult old man, and deaf. There is no reason, I think, to ignore any longer the fact that Koraes' "correction of the common dialect," seen in perspective, is a belated offspring of Atticism, perhaps not immediately recognizable.[6]

[5] Achilles Rose, *Christian Greece and Living Greek*, New York, 1898, chap. 1, p. 9.

[6] It is worth recalling that G. Mistriotis (1840-1916), while admitting that his generation still practiced, or had a feeling for, the

On the language question, as on the question of religion, Koraes preferred to advocate a "lukewarm" compromise (with the pejorative meaning in *Revelation* 3:16), a compromise lame in theory and faltering in practice, without taking into consideration that these are the only areas where there is no room for compromise. In the end, for most people he muddied the waters both in language and religion with his contradictory views, or his retrogressions, in a maze of encyclopedic loquacity where the eager student searches in vain to find an exit. If every man's undeniable linguistic theory is in his writing, then the theory of the famous emender of Strabo is to be found in the way he writes. In the well-known letter to Alexander Vassiliou which contains Koraes' digressions on language (from

---

common language, nevertheless maintained that the generation following his, "our children"—the "enlightened ones"—"ask for an explanation every time we introduce common words. Therefore the language of the Klephts and those fighting the Turks does not yet enchant the ears nor move the hearts of the new educated and civilized generation. *The common language of today is not that which was created by the enslaved Greeks in their huts in order to express their natural needs, but the language that was shaped by the liberated nation through its best minds, under the national leadership of Koraes*" ("Εκθεσις τῶν πεπραγμένων ὑπὸ τῆς κεντρικῆς ἐπιτροπῆς ἐπὶ τῆς ἑκαντονταετηρίδος τοῦ Σολωμοῦ [*Report of the Acts of the Central Committee on the Occasion of Solomos' Centenary*], Zakynthos, 1903, p. 58). It is apparent from the very beginning that the learned class or the "educated and civilized generation" that became the self-ordained leaders of the country—some of these self-ordained even before setting foot in Greece—wanted to deprive the enslaved nation not only of its language (they shaped their own "common" language "under the national leadership of Koraes") but also of its freedom (they constituted "the liberated nation"). As things have turned out, they did not prove to be so naive in their calculations.

which all the quotations so far have been taken), after the short greeting, we encounter the following ominous beginning in the first sentence: Ὑέτιος ὁ τῆς ἐν Γαλλίᾳ Ἀβρίγκης Ἐπίσκοπος . . . for: "Huet, Bishop of Avranches." It is our acoustically well-known hubbub that, in another context, Koraes invokes in reference to those who fill their writings with these pedantic purisms that "twist the tongue and shatter the ears of the listeners." The one thing brings the other: as we have said, the lame theory brought on a faltering practice, namely Koraes' own writing, and also that of the heirs to that sort of writing; just as the theory of Solomos *is* his writing, and at the same time is the touchstone for the heirs to his writing. The proof of the pudding is in the eating.

Solomos attacked Koraes in his *Dialogos* without distinguishing him from the character of the Pedant. He saw that the faults of the learned tradition lasted two thousand years and that it is almost impossible for someone who had given himself unrepentantly to this tradition for a period of time to retract. The harm had already been done by then, and, with the centuries, whole icebergs of works written in the secondary language (Dante's *secundaria locutio*) had accumulated, so that no one could eradicate them with one stroke of the pen or could bury them from one day to the next. That inheritance remained, with its good and its bad elements, its dry wood and its sprouting shoots, indeed growing worse during Solomos' time, with its many scribblers, collators, translators, and messengers or torch-bearers—a real typographical inflation—who at that time flew in from the ends of the world to "enlighten" our enslaved nation. The overwhelming majority of these pure patriots (so many gave their lives for the struggle) denigrated the language of the nation they wanted to "enlighten" or never used it, and so left the country "wronged in its mastery of the language given it by nature," according to Solomos. Koraes characteristically notes at one point (again in the same text): "And then, for what ignoramuses do we write? Of course not for the vulgar populace that doesn't even have cognizance of our presence in this world." I think the feeling here was mutual: did Koraes in fact have any more "cognizance" of the presence of the "vulgar populace" in this world?

This constitutes the error of the learned tradition. Vulgar populace or not, the people who speak the same language speak their national language. And the written language is nothing else—as we have said many times—but the written expression of the living or spoken language, in order to serve more quickly or more efficiently certain needs that the spoken language cannot reach. With the living language as a basis, one can and must cultivate the written language, and no one can find fault with the content of that language, whether it be difficult or incomprehensible, as long as one follows in writing the form of that spoken language. This very form also constitutes the basic form of that language spoken by the populace, vulgar or not: the language of all of us. One is free with regard to the content of the language; one is not free with regard to its form. Freedom is in the spirit, not the letter. The letter of a language must be common. This facilitates the circulation of knowledge or culture, and raises the general level, according to the law of communicating vessels. The letter of one's language must be the letter of all, of the vulgar populace and of those not belonging to the vulgar populace, and in that letter one can be original or achieve greatness with the content of one's writing, and one can become as difficult as one wants without ceasing to belong to everyone, or at least without ceasing theoretically to be within reach of everyone. Whoever wants to understand is free to do so. The letter of the language has been followed. One is responsible for the form, not the content. The error, then, the failure of understanding, does not reside in the writer but in his audience, vulgar or not vulgar. Otherwise, if one writes in a language *other* than that of one's nurse—Dante said *nutricem imitans*—one is responsible for any failure of understanding, whether from form or content.

There was no need, then, for the "vulgar populace" to have "cognizance" of Koraes' presence in this world. It was Koraes who should have had "cognizance" of the presence of the "vulgar populace." From the form of his writing it seems he did not. To the question of the Pedant in the *Dialogos*: "Do you know Greek?" the Poet answers with the question: "Do you know the Greeks?" Illiterate Makriyannis will say that "Man makes the lights, the lights do not make man." Greek for the Pedant is ancient Greek, "which has stopped being spoken," according to Koraes. "The forms of Greek words," which means ancient Greek words, belong on one side; on the other side belong "our own," which it seems are not Greek. Solomos puts things back in their proper place, making the distinction between Greek (ancient) and the Greeks (modern), between the ancient Greek language that has stopped "being spoken" and modern man who has not stopped speaking. This man needs to write the language he speaks. That is what he means by: "Do you know the Greeks?"

The *Dialogos* is full of references to the verb "enlighten," as in "enlighten the country," and to "lights"—the same "lights" that enraged Makriyannis—and the references are all directed against the silly attempt of the Pedant, that is to say, of the learned tradition, to educate the country at that time according to the models of Western enlightenment and its classical ideals: "We have seen the benefit you gave to the Greek Revolution with your lights." Solomos categorically denies Koraes' compromising "correcting of the language" and cries out: "the forms of words, when they are in common use, are not subject to change by any one under the pretext of correction." Solomos accepts Koraes' pronouncements regarding embellishing "as much as possible the language we were nursed on with our milk," "beautifying the language" and "beautifying their speech," but, as a true artificer of the language, Solomos separates these pronouncements from the unacceptable "correcting" of the common language; he naturally supports them in the *Dialogos* with the indispensable reservation that "the basis on which we must beautify our language must be today's language."

We cannot know whether Solomos read the letter to A. Vassiliou. But one thing we can know is that the *Dialogos* closely follows Koraes' terminology about the language. As an all-time symbol and type of artificially "correcting" a living language, Solomos takes the first verse of the *Divine Comedy*: "Nel mezzo del cammin di nostra vita," and "latinizes" (his term) Dante's Italian to: "In medio cammini nostrae vitae." Of this offense, Solomos says: "Here is the verse corrected and the country enlightened!"

We must elucidate one point with regard to the *Dia-*

logos. Because Koraes did not write "Hellinisti" (ancient Greek) or because he ridiculed those "purely Hellenizing," does not mean that he was not responsible, with his contradictory position, for the third and last unleashing of the learned tradition, and for the establishment of the *secundaria* of Dante, the secondary written language of the 19th century, *katharevousa.* Nor does it mean that he is excused for not having written the language that Solomos and Makriyannis wrote. I also consider Koraes' metaphor for the national language purposeless and misleading: "the orphaned and unhappy daughter of another more perfect language." Orphanhood and unhappiness belong to human beings, not languages. Sometimes a human being may even bring on his own misery; languages can do nothing of the sort.

The Greek language did not decline, did not become barbarized, did not have anything happen to it, but on the contrary was a unique and maybe unrepeatable phenomenon. "Besides, it is something unique in the world: this panorama of a language spoken and written for three thousand years, which, though passing through different phases from time to time, has nevertheless remained to this very day one and the same, precise and clear throughout all these centuries," rightly says G. Hadzidakis in a short survey of the Greek language that introduces the modern Greek translation of Liddell and Scott's *Dictionary* (Μέγα Λεξικὸν τῆς Ἑλληνικῆς Γλώσσης, Athens, 1910, 2 vols.). Moreover, today's language is not a "daughter," nor was the ancient one "another" language, as Koraes believed. The language is one, a *mortally immortal* language—that is the miracle—the modern coming out of the old, that which was spoken by people for thousands of years, from generation to generation, that was constantly changed and shaped by being spoken without interruption, without ever dying, until in its present phase it became one with our mother language, itself a starting point for who knows what new creations or what future changes. The fable of language, like the fable of life, never ends, especially that of a venerable language like ours. The fable will follow its destiny as long as there are mouths to tell it and young children to hear it.

What hindered the process of the living language becoming the written language of the country was viewed by Solomos as an impediment to "the ways in which knowledge flows," that is, an impediment to the country's education; and he struggled generously to bring reason to those who contributed to the continuation or even perpetuity of this severe iniquity. He was afraid that the anomaly would become a chronic disease and that any hope of organically surpassing this linguistic anastomosis would be lessened and would eventually disappear, as long as the faulty system continued to exist. A transfer of the live word to written symbols is indispensable to every country with a certain civilization; the written language is used for the quick and effective communication between those speaking the same language who want to reach an understanding for a thousand and one individual, group, state, educational, theoretical, or practical purposes. The center sends messages to the periphery, the periphery to the center, and a good circulation keeps alive the whole organism of a society, both in the body proper and in its members. In the case of institutions like the administration, the army, education, and the press, the written language in which these will express their spirit or reveal their intent is important, as well as in what written language the whole people will be forced to express its own sovereign will or its group reactions.

In Greece at no time have we been able to find the only natural solution to the question of the written language, the solution of Solomos or Dante. I mean we have not been able to do so as a whole, as a Greek society. Several years after the *Dialogos*—maybe in 1842—Solomos wrote to Tertsetis (in a letter that was never found in the Italian original, but only in a Greek translation): "Twenty-one years ago today Greece broke her chains. This day of the Annunciation is a day for joy and for tears. Joy for the future, tears for past slavery. And what about today? Corruption is so general and has such deep roots that it is distracting. Only when the causes of corruption have been eliminated for good will we be able to have a moral renaissance. Then our future will be great, when everything will be based on morality, when justice will triumph, when letters will be cultivated not for vain show but for the good of the people who need education and a culture that isn't pedantic" ("*Panathinaia,*" Vol. 18, 1909, p. 260). Wise and bitter thoughts when one thinks that from that time on things have remained static, at the crossroads of Solomos' observation.

Solomos struggled generously to bring reason to the opposite faction. He recognized that everyone's final aim was the good of the country. Though he speaks harshly in the *Dialogos* about the learned tradition, he declares that he has "a quick lip but not a bad heart," and he begs forgiveness, addressing his opponent as "beloved brother." To the Pedant he says explicitly: "Both you and I are fighting for the truth, but consider seriously whether by looking for truth in that way, you may not be deceived by embracing a phantom image of it. Come to your senses; think what harm is done by the language you write. . . . It is no shame for a man to recognize his mistake, in fact every honest man will praise you, and I will give your forehead the kiss of peace." He compares the learned tradition to the Turkish dynast of that time; he sees freedom "beginning to step on Turkish heads," and the language "soon about to step on the heads of the pedants . . . without ever turning back should a pedant croak or a Turk bark; because for me the two are the same." The insinuation against the learned tradition is deadly and unforgettable, as will be seen below. During the period of Solomos' youthful optimism—he wrote the *Dialogos*, as we have said, at about the age of 25—he thought the problem would be solved automatically with the end of slavery in Greece, and he threatened the opposite faction as follows: "I'm giving you the news that your reign over Greece has ended with the reign of the Turks. It has ended, and maybe you will curse the day of the Revolution." We saw in Solomos' letter to Tertsetis (June 1, 1833)—if my supposition is correct—that he soon realized his haste, and admitted the small prudence (*poco prudenza*) that the *Dialogos* showed on this point.

The comparison with the Turk is not just a figure of speech in Solomos' view. He who puts obstacles in "the ways by which knowledge flows" is truly a traitor to his country, since the progress of the country depends on the language. In Solomos' eyes, one must be a Turk, or else a pedant, in order to impede, for example, the brilliant beginnings of the written language in Crete in the 17th century, beginnings that stopped with the enslavement of the island by the Turks in 1669 and that brought a wave of Cretan refugees to the Ionian islands (among them the ancestors of the poet).[7] For Solomos the learned tradition, by its social presence, brought on the same impediment to the natural development of the nation's voice. In that period, whoever aimed at any distinction in the fields of art or science never wrote in the common language; and it would be appropriate to say about them what Dante says in *De Vulgari Eloquentia* about the Sardinians of his time, namely, that "they do not seem to have a common language of their own, and they imitate Latin like monkeys imitate men" ("Soli sine proprio vulgari esse videntur, grammaticam tamquam simie homines imitantes"). As a parallel to what was happening in Greece, Fauriel notes that "in Italy those who had any pretensions to the honors and respect acquired through science and talent had to write in Latin. They seriously believed themselves to be the heirs of Virgil and Horace and disdained the poets who wrote in the common language."[8]

This craze reached the point in both East and West where some indigenous texts like the *Chanson de Roland* or the *Erotokritos* were translated into Latin or archaistic Greek. Even Solomos' "Hymn" (1823), which became the national anthem after the expulsion of King Otho (1862),

[7] There was a Solomos in Chanea in 1372. Domenico Centranico took on the name Salomone in Venice in 1027, and from there we can go as far back as the Barbolani, who migrated to the city of St. Mark from Salerno in 715 (see Romily Jenkins, *Dionysios Solomos*, Cambridge, 1940, pp. 2-3).

[8] *Dante et les origines de la langue et de la littérature Italiennes*, Paris, 1854, Vol. 1, p. 3.

ran into the danger of being replaced by another "of a nobler and higher language." It is characteristic, in relation to what we are saying, that a circle of learned men around Janus Laskaris induced Pope Leo X to open a Greek Gymnasium in Rome during the 16th century for the purpose of preserving Greek and having it taught in Italy by Greeks. This circle was afraid, no more and no less, that Greek would one day disappear completely from Greece. This means that they saw the Greek language as lost exactly where it was alive and in the process of being shaped—that is, among the enslaved Greeks—and they saw it as substantial there where it actually remained static and uninvolved in life. These are some of the things that can happen when one has—as in Greece or Italy—the burden of two great languages and two great literatures.

In any case, the identification of the Pedant with the Turk was not forgotten. Almost half a century after the first publication of Solomos' *Dialogos*, George Hadzidakis (1848-1941) conceived the idea of questioning the authenticity of the text,[9] and ever since, the learned tradition has followed this contrived fallacy (i.e., "Is the *Dialogos* authentic?"), even when Solomos' handwritten excerpts of MS No. 12 were found in the Masonic Lodge of Zakynthos. Hadzidakis was aiming at establishing two things: (1) that possibly the *Dialogos* was not authentic, and (2) that Solomos' attack was not directed against Koraes. To Solomos' "If some Pedant croaks," Hadzidakis comments: "But he meant then those recommending the use of the

[9] Ἀπάντησις εἰς τὰ τοῦ Κ. Κρουμβάχερ (*Answer to K. Krumbacher*), Athens, 1905, p. 679.

pure ancient language, not men like Koraes, Oikonomos, and others."[10]

Koraes laid the foundations, as we have said, for the study of the modern language and its texts (medieval and modern) not in order to study the national language itself, with its "beastly coarseness," but rather in order to help the study of the ancient language, the "knowledge" of which he felt so necessary for hastening "the progress of the Greek renaissance" (as he writes to his friend A. Vassiliou). Hadzidakis, on the other hand, became the founder of modern Greek linguistics: that is to say, he not only brought the science of language to Greece (many could have done that), but he was the first to define the method and to trace the historic outline that has been followed ever since by all scientific research, Greek or foreign, in the national language (and in this his contribution was unique). Koraes was the first to teach the importance of the modern language, even if he did it in order to help the "knowledge" of the ancient. He tells us: "One of the ways to help the teaching of ancient Greek is to compare it to that common language on which we were nursed with our mother's milk"—this naturally with all the philological and scientific consequences of such a comparison. Koraes' glory is summed up in this remark, which seems so obvious today, but was not at all so in his time.

Hadzidakis' glory—no small one and exclusively his—was to start from Koraes' parallel and, with the then newly created science of linguistics, to prove beyond a doubt the descent of the medieval and modern language from the older *koine* (let us leave aside the disagreements of the

[10] Καὶ πάλιν περὶ τοῦ Γλωσσικοῦ Ζητήματος (*Again on the Language Question*), Athens, 1907, p. 100.

linguists about the exact definition of the *koine*) and to establish this fertile lesson as a scientific principle. He was the first to undertake the scientific investigation of the modern language, and with the help of the laws of his science, was in a better position than Koraes to teach (and to put into practice) the first and greatest linguistic commandment upon which the expressive flowering of any language depends: namely, that a written language means the written expression of the oral or mother language. Like Koraes, Hadzidakis took the wrong course. From the moment when he hesitated and chose to advocate the theoretically shipwrecked case of the learned tradition in the question of the written language, Hadzidakis wastefully squandered his scientific capacity in sparrings unworthy of the father of modern Greek linguistics; and his deviation from the imaginary line of decorum and moderation—as was also true of his opponents (e.g., I. Psycharis)—clouded his mind (and his heart) to the point where he called one of Solomos' most famous works "that insipid *Dialogos*."[11] The *Dialogos* says: "There are two flames, teacher, one in the mind, the other in the heart, that light up in some men, who use different means at different times to enjoy the same results." Mind and heart keep the scales in balance; they must not be disturbed by turbulence; otherwise the weighing comes out faulty.

Hadzidakis, however, tried to sully a higher spirit like that of Solomos with the wily insinuation that since Solomos himself had not fought or taken any physical risks in the War of Independence, as D. Ypsilantis or A. Mavrocordatos "and others like them had—all of them *using* with Koraes the *written language*" (in other words, those

[11] Κρουμβάχερ *(Answer to K. Krumbacher), loc.cit.*

who like Koraes *did not write the common language*)—Solomos had no right to put in the *Dialogos* "those improperly said words" about the Pedant and those like him, namely that "our people are shedding their blood beneath the Cross in order to make us free, and he and those like him are fighting as a reward to deprive them of their language." Solomos, according to Hadzidakis, "living in full peace and security, accused men who were fighting and endangering themselves for the nation of trying to eliminate the language of the nation." Poor virtue, you are led astray hiding "in mountains and in dens and caves of the earth." And Hadzidakis concludes with this language of Babel ("quella lingua Babelica") that he used: "As I read through that insipid *Dialogos* years ago and thought about the unfairness done to men who didn't deserve it, *I remember well* [my italics] that I smiled about the weakness and slippery character of human nature" (*ibid.*, p. 679). Truly, human nature has weaknesses and its slippery side.

Judging Solomos' *Dialogos* insipid, Hadzidakis was himself judged. To what advantage? It is with real distress that one writes today about great teachers who, with their talent, with their forcefulness, and with their labor, all sought the good of the country, where the influence of an evil demon, it would seem, never let the flock rightly enjoy all the good things that these shepherds intended for it. There is no possibility that some day an impartial generation will emerge. And I do not mean only in Greece. Nor does what we call "impartial history" exist. History is what we are. We shall always be an "adulterous and sinful generation" (Mark 8:38), and from there, from our despair and our old age, our hope and youth will be singled out each time in a Solomos or a Dante.

We must not be amazed that a philologist like Koraes or a linguist like Hadzidakis taught different things about the language than those taught by Dante or Solomos. Nothing prevented them from teaching the same things; the appraisal was not for them a question of scientific integrity or the command of truth; it just so happened. We know of philologists and linguists who taught the same lesson as Dante and Solomos without violating the laws of their respective sciences, or without betraying the truth. The problem lies elsewhere. For the philologist or the scientist, language is a theory, an external matter, a phenomenon, and finally an object *for study.* But for the poet—as for the people, whose relation to the language is the bond of need—language is action. Not an external matter, not an object, but a subject *for liberation*: something that does not hold you by the brain or by your reflective capacity, but by the guts, one might say. As the poet goes his great or small way, he feels the resistance of the language. Language is the poet's element; in it he soars high or falls headlong, and, contrary to Kant's dove, he never imagines he could fly better in a vacuum. I understand perfectly Hadzidakis' description of Solomos as "a poet of great importance, but totally inexperienced in the Greek language and its history," considering the perspective from which he viewed and knew the subject. One also understands his surprise that "Koraes, Doukas, Vamvas, Koumas, Genadios, Gazis, Oikonomos, and so many other *fathers of the nation*" (*ibid.*, p. 816) could ever be considered harmful to the progress of the language, as they are by implication when Solomos exclaims in the *Dialogos*: "O Pedants! Are these the lessons you teach the people, wanting to enlighten them? You could enlighten them just as well by throwing a handful of dust in their eyes!" His surprise is natural. Without being the editor of Koraes' Ἑλληνικὴ Βιβλιοθήκη (*Greek Library*), and in comparison with Hadzidakis' linguistic competence, Solomos was "totally inexperienced," one might say, in the science of linguistics or in historical method; but in spite of this Solomos remained a fountain of wisdom in the matter of the language.

Perhaps he did not lay a foundation stone for the knowledge of Greek, as Koraes did, nor did he quarry medieval and modern Greek with the scientific sledgehammer of Hadzidakis—this was not his job—but he did something different, something tied more closely to the collective or individual soul of the enslaved nation that was being resurrected: he became the legislator of the written language. Solomos will remain once and for all, "now and in the future," for the collective and the individual soul, "both personal and public," the one who settled the debt that weighed on our language from the distant time of Atticism. He rid us of the disburdening ordinance ("seisachthia") of our language—"liberating us from the weight," as Aristotle goes on to say of Solon in *The Constitution of Athens* (VI, I)—when in the humiliation and despair of slavery, certain learned Greeks dreamed that they would capture in the written word the golden bird that had flown from the spoken word, without first calculating that the words of a language are not "whited sepulchers," but the cradles of life.

Solomos did not study or write the history of the Greek language, but with his writing he acquired a place in its history. And along with the people who unceasingly give shape to the language, only those who acquire by their writing a place in the history of their language can finally be said to exist for it. Before writers such as Dante and Solomos, there was less spiritual room in the language. With their writing and the place it earned for them in the history of the language, they bequeathed to others a voice more alive and sharp. The language that they left behind occupied a broader area on the maps of the spirit or the psyche. How many can be said to have gained such annexations for their language?

More than one hundred years after the *Dialogos* of Solomos was first published (1859), we find ourselves still burdened by the problem of the written language, a problem still far from solved. To be sure, we have progressed slightly, especially if we take into consideration that—since the years of Atticism—the first attempt as a nation to follow (or not to follow) the path of the *Dialogos* in the matter of the written language has been made in our own times. During the past century the hopes for a solution of the problem in keeping with the ideas of Solomos have been based less on substance than on statistics. This distinction does not mean that the hopes do not exist, and it does not in the least mean that these hopes are vain.

So much for the student who follows the linguistic position of the *Dialogos* and the *De Vulgari Eloquentia*. A follower of the learned tradition need only substitute the word "fear" for the word "hope." His position would be the opposite.

Emmanuel Stais, of Kythera, one of the first who took it upon himself to "remove the critical mind of Greece from its swaddling clothes" (in the words of Polylas) noted with far-reaching vision in his pamphlet "Κριτική.

Ὁ Λάμπρος τοῦ Σολωμοῦ" (*The Lambros of Solomos: a Critique*):[12] ". . . and at last I saw the nation being directed unswervingly toward *that* road . . . which the word of its Prophet had revealed since the day its freedom dawned." Further on, with even greater critical acumen, he wrote: "It was enough for them to listen to Solomos' general concept about the language, a concept that he not only expounded but also put into practice in his writing as no one else had been able to do." And still further on, this time from another angle and with a positive viewpoint unusual for his times: "People with opposing views (and many with opposing interests) found themselves at the same time at the head of the school, of the community, and of the whole national movement, and they gave it a different direction than the one he wanted to give it." Emmanuel Stais had digested the broader teaching of Solomos: "The nation must learn to consider as national that which is true." He was able to add, over and above the linguistic problem, words of a kind that had not been heard in the world since the time of the apostle Paul: ". . . I am convinced that nationalism must yield to Christianity, that is, to love for humanity, and enlightened by this feeling, I consider without any passion both the superiority of the Greek to the foreigner and the superiority of the foreigner to the Greek." This is what Emmanuel Stais had to offer in publishing the first notable critical analysis of Solomos' *Lambros*.

Solomos established the form of the written language once and for all, both for poetry and for prose. His language is the golden rule. With his *Dialogos* we have the

[12] Published in Athens six full years (1853) before the *Dialogos* and the *Prolegomena* of Polylas.

first written example, or the prototype, for Greek prose writing, completed and perfected in an unrivalled way a little later (1826-1829) with the enigmatic *Γυναίκα τῆς Ζάκυθος* (*The Woman of Zakynthos*). The excerpt from *Romeo and Juliet* (v, i, 42-48) included in his *Dialogos* at the point where, in speaking of those who "write in that obscure way," he says that "they should be compared to those people who, in order to make a living, sell poison," and recalls how "Shakespeare so excellently describes the workshop of one of them"—this excerpt can be characterized in its manner of expression as the *ovum mundi*, the egg of the universe, out of which have come the best specimens (the few that we have) of our modern literature. This workshop and Shakespeare's words "remind" Solomos of "the manner in which the books of the learned pedants were written." Let me first cite Shakespeare's text:

And in his needy shop a tortoise hung,
An alligator stuff'd, and other skins
Of ill-shap'd fishes; and about his shelves
A beggarly account of empty boxes,
Green earthen pots, bladders, and musty seeds,
Remnants of packthread, and old cakes of roses
Were thinly scatter'd, to make up a show.

And now Solomos' translation:

" Ἐκρέμονταν ἀπὸ τὸ πατερὸ τοῦ φτωχότατου ἐργαστηριοῦ μία ξεροχελώνα, ἕνας κροκόδειλος ἀχερωμένος καὶ ἄλλα δερμάτια ἄσχημων ψαριῶν· ἦτον τριγύρου πολλὰ συρτάρια ἀδειανὰ μὲ ἐπιγραφές, ἀγγειὰ ἀπὸ χοντρόπηλο πράσινο, ἦτον φοῦσκες, ἦτον βρωμόχορτα

παλιωμένα, κακομοιριασμένα δεμάτια βοῦρλα, παλιὰ κομμάτια ἀπὸ διαφόρων λογιῶν ἰατρικά, ἀριὰ σπαρμένα ἐδῶ κι' ἐκεῖ γιὰ νὰ προσκαλέσουν τὸν ἀγοραστή."

This passage is, in miniature, the arsenal that supplied the weapons for everyone who has fought—each according to his ability—to preserve intact his own expression, from Sikelianos to Seferis.

The two virtues mentioned in the *Dialogos*, virtues which Solomos never forgot—"is there anything else in my mind but freedom and language?"—these two virtues found their superlative expression in his work: the one in his early *Hymn* (1823), the other in his early *Dialogos* (1824). At that time the great dark cloud of isolation had not yet covered the poet of Ἐλεύθεροι Πολιορκημένοι (*The Free Besieged*), as happened later, when, as Polylas puts it: ". . . Solomos was no longer showing his writings to anyone." For as long as a Greek language exists, the *Dialogos*, together with the Ὕμνος εἰς τὴν Ἐλευθερίαν (*Hymn to Liberty*), will occupy unshakably the deep center of nationhood: "il centro profondo della nazionalità."

With his writing Solomos demonstrated that the common language (naturalis) can compete with the artificial one (artificialis), just as Dante had proved that the common language of his time could compete with Latin. Solomos understood that the written language must be a written formulation of the spoken one, and that in following this principle, the writer is free to use—as Polylas appropriately puts it—both "the royal treasury of the ancient language and the poor purse of the demotiki." Solomos wrote on the resolute foundation of the living language, today's common language, the blessed spoken word that offers the unimaginable intellectual advantage of having behind it the three-thousand-year-old richness of one of the basic languages of the world. To the unambiguous lesson of Solomos—and of Dante—concerning the written language, we must outspokenly answer with a simple "Yea, yea; Nay, nay: for whatsoever is more than these cometh of evil" (Matthew 5:37).

Bertrand Bouvier

2. *Calvos in Geneva*

Registration District:	*Louth, County of Lincoln*
When and where died:	*Third November 1869, the High Holme, Louth*
Name and Surname:	*Andrea Kalvo*
Age:	*77 years*
Rank or Profession:	*Professor of Languages and Mathematics*

I DO NOT know of a more poignant document than this to illustrate the haughty solitude and the bitterness that marked the life of Andreas Calvos. His death certificate,[1] established in a foreign language, does not mention his faraway country and, as did his contemporaries, refuses him the title of poet.

Calvos spent all the years of his life as a stranger on earth, whether in Italy, in England, in Switzerland, or even among his own countrymen. His Greek poetical work—two thin collections of poems published at the age of 32 and 34, the first one in Geneva, the second in Paris—seems to have aroused but little interest among the people of his time. Though a number of his odes were published again in Athens in 1864, five years before his death, true interest in his poetry was manifested only at the end of the 19th and the beginning of the 20th centuries, and was especially due to the interest shown by Palamas. But it is the heirs of Palamas, and in some measure those who contradicted his poetic practice who, we believe, have done full justice to Calvos by recognizing in him one of the creators of modern Greek poetry, together with Solomos.

[1] For the complete text, see A. Indianos, "'Ο *τάφος τοῦ Κάλβου στὴν 'Αγγλία*," *Νέα 'Εστία*, 68 (1960), 203.

In fact, a return to Calvos[2] is one of the characteristics of the generation of the 1930's.[3] Critics, literary historians, linguists, and poets have, each in his own field and according to various methods, tried to study and understand the personality and work of the Zantiot poet.

In 1946, the Athenian periodical *Nea Estia* summed up their research and reflections; anyone intending to approach or go deeply into the subject will find this issue still indispensable.[4] To limit ourself to the major contributions, let us mention that thanks to the biographers of Calvos, George Zoras first among them, the main lines of his life are now known, and a number of particular problems now solved;[5] that thanks to the incomparable comparatist Constantine Dimaras, the sources of the inspira-

[2] The expression belongs to C. Th. Dimaras, "'*Ἐπιστροφὴ πρὸς τὸν Κάλβο*,'' *Ἐλεύθερον Βῆμα*, June 19, 1937.

[3] As was judiciously observed by G. Theotokas (*Πνευματικὴ πορεία*, Athens, 1961, pp. 230-31): "*Μιὰ ἀπὸ τὶς προσφορὲς τῆς γενεᾶς αὐτῆς εἶναι ὅτι κατόρθωσε, ἤδη ἀπὸ τὰ νεανικά της χρόνια, νὰ καλλιεργήσει καὶ νὰ διαπλατύνει τὴ συνείδηση τῶν γραμμάτων μας ὥστε νὰ χωρέσει μέσα της, ἀβίαστα, ἁρμονικά, τὸ Σολωμὸ καὶ τὸν Κὰλβο, τὸν Παλαμᾶ καὶ τὸν Καβάφη, τὸ Σικελιανὸ καὶ τὴ νεώτερη ποίηση τοῦ Σεφέρη καὶ τοῦ Ἐλύτη.*"

[4] *Νέα Ἑστία*, 40 (Christmas 1946). Reprinted with important addenda in the same periodical, 68 (September 1960).

[5] "'*Ἀνδρέας Κάλβος* (1792-1869)," *Νέα Ἑστία*, *ibid.*, pp. 3-86. The study by N. B. Tomadakis, "'*Ὁ Ἀνδρέας Κάλβος ἀπὸ Λιβόρνου εἰς Φλωρεντίαν*," *Ἀφιέρωμα εἰς Κωνσταντῖνον Ἄμαντον*, Athens, 1940, pp. 163-96, remains the model of research on a definite period of the poet's life. It is also to George Zoras that we owe the best text available today of the twenty odes of Calvos; it is based on the original editions of 1824 and 1826, the two contemporary French translations being printed in front of the Greek text, and it contains a critical appendix that sums up the state of our knowledge (*Κάλβου: Ὠιδαὶ μετὰ τῆς πρώτης γαλλικῆς μεταφράσεως ὑπὸ* St. Julien *καὶ* Pauthier de Censay, Athens, 1962).

tion of Calvos have been identified and his situation in neo-hellenic and European letters defined.[6] Let us also mention that George Seferis and Odysseas Elytis have shown how exemplary and profoundly actual the poet's quest was, in spite of his errors.[7]

Yet specialists themselves agree that our information about Calvos is incomplete, concerning both details of his adventurous and secretive career and the genesis of his work, which remained isolated. We must therefore be satisfied that under such conditions the study of Calvos still arouses such interest. Recent research has proved that much use remains to be made of certain stores of manuscripts, archives, and even some printed matter. For example, Mario Vitti, while re-editing the Italian works of Foscolo's friend, had the good fortune to discover a capital text whose existence was known only through an allusion by the author and which was believed to have been written in Italian. It is a fragment of Calvos' ode to Napoleon, composed in 1811 in Greek hendecasyllabic verse, in a style that strikingly foreshadows that of the *Lyre* and the *New Odes*.[8] It was Vitti again who grouped together all

[6] "*Ρωμαντικὰ σημειώματα. Οἱ πηγὲς τῆς ἔμπνευσης τοῦ Κάλβου*," *Νέα Ἑστία*, 68 (1960), 270-300.

[7] G. Seferis, *Ἀπορίες διαβάζοντας τὸν Κάλβο* [1937], *Πρόλογος γιὰ μιὰ ἔκδοση τῶν "Ὠδῶν* [1941], *Κάλβος, 1960*. (These three texts are gathered in the volume *Δοκιμές*, 2nd edition, Athens, 1962, pp. 21-28, 145-72, 369-89); and O. Elytis, "*Ἡ ἀληθινὴ φυσιογνωμία καὶ ἡ λυρικὴ τόλμη τοῦ Ἀνδρέα Κάλβου*" [1940], *Νέα Ἑστία*, 68 (1960), 240-69.

[8] M. Vitti, *A. Kalvos e i suoi scritti in italiano*, Naples, 1960, pp. 51-53 and 325-28; revised version: "*Ἀπόσπασμα ἀπὸ ἄτιτλο ποίημα* (1811) *τοῦ Ἀνδρέα Κάλβου*," *Νέα Ἑστία*, 72 (1962), 1,084-86. Very recently G. Zoras submitted this untitled fragment to close scrutiny and concluded that it was unquestionably by Calvos

the letters Calvos received between 1813 and 1820, thus providing precious documentation about the poet's London period, a decisive period since it preceded the time of composition and publication of the odes.[9] For their part, researchers like A. Indianos and C. Porphyris have published some revealing documents from Calvos' political file.[10] These are a timely reminder that work like that of Calvos, entirely dedicated to Virtue and Liberty, was not generated in some kind of aseptic medium (which could be that of belles-lettres) but took sides in the merciless struggle between the forces of liberalism and those of conservatism at the time of the Holy Alliance.

Our aim in this essay is to provide similar information on the Genevan years of Calvos. Let these notes be considered a mere preliminary to an overall study on Calvos and Switzerland, which remains to be done. Indeed, the keen article by N. Bees, "Calvos' Works and Days in Switzerland," which appeared in the *Proceedings of the Academy of Athens*, does not exhaust the subject; yet it constitutes, with the precise facts it brings to light and the hypotheses it formulates, an excellent basis for further investigation.[11]

---

but that it could not be identified with his ode to Napoleon (" 'Ανδρέα Κάλβου *ἀπόσπασμα ἀγνώστου ποιήματος*," Παρνασσός, n.s., 11 [1969], 511-35.)

[9] Πηγὲς *γιὰ τὴ βιογραφία τοῦ* Κάλβου (*ἐπιστολὲς* 1813-1820), Thessaloniki, 1963 (supplement no. 15 to the periodical 'Ελληνικά).

[10] A. C. Indianos, *Ἄγνωστες σελίδες ἀπὸ τὴ ζωὴ καὶ τὸ ἔργο τοῦ* 'Ανδρέα Κάλβου, Nicosia, 1960, pp. 9-22; C. Porphyris, " 'Ο 'Ανδρέας Κάλβος *στέλεχος τῶν* Καρμπονάρων," 'Επιθεώρηση *τέχνης*, 18 (1963), 372-85.

[11] N. A. Bees, "Κάλβου *ἔργα καὶ ἡμέραι ἐν* 'Ελβετία," Πραγματεῖαι *τῆς* 'Ακαδημίας 'Αθηνῶν, Vol. 22, no. 2 (Athens, 1958), 1-24.

To begin, let us establish a few points of chronology. We know that Calvos left England in the fall of 1820 and spent the winter in Tuscany. Accused by the secret police of dealings with the Carbonari, he was expelled from Florence on April 22, 1821, with orders to leave the Grand Duchy of Tuscany within three days. The British ambassador intervened in vain against these measures, although Calvos had asserted his rights as a British subject, having been born in the Heptanese.[12] On the 22nd of May 1821, a month later, Calvos' name was recorded in the police register of foreigners in Geneva; the certificate of registration given him on this date was regularly renewed until the 4th of December 1824, on which date his passport was given back to him to allow him to travel to Lausanne. On the 13th of January 1825, the minister plenipotentiary of His Majesty the King of England to the Swiss Confederation granted Calvos a passport with which he travelled to France.[13]

I personally verified, in the State Archives of Geneva, the particulars of Calvos' stay. They are of great interest, since they establish with certainty that our poet resided in the city of Calvin for three years and eight months, that he claimed the title and occupation of "professor of languages," and that his dwellings were near the Place Saint-Gervais.[14] I like underlining this detail of social and spir-

[12] C. Porphyris, pp. 378-79.

[13] A. Indianos, p. 16.

[14] I have noted four occasions on which Calvos is mentioned in official documents of Geneva, two in the Foreigners' Register and two in the Census books of February 1822. Here is the exact transcription of the first two:

a) *N° d'ordre: 9090. Date de la permission: May 22. Renouvellement: vu le 22 aout 21* xx *(visa). Noms: Calbo. Prénoms: André.*

itual topography: Calvos chose to live on the right bank of the Rhone, around the corner from the house where Jean-Jacques Rousseau had spent his youth, right in the busy suburb of Genevan watch-making and calico-printing craftsmen, where the traditions of republicanism and

---

Age: — Profession: Profess. lang. Patrie: Zantes. Nombre d'individus: — Pièces déposées: passeport. Domicile à Genève, Rue: St Gervais, Maison: Aguet. Observations: [The two crosses by the visa, under the heading of renewals, indicate the extensions accorded every three months (November 22, 1821 and February 22, 1822).] (Archives d'Etat de Genève, permissions de séjour, registre étrangers Dd, vol. n° 6, année 1821, fol. 230^{v}-231^{r}.)

b) *Ancien N°: 9090. N° d'ordre: 1869. Date de la permission: 22 May. Renouvellement:* ||| |||| ||. *Noms: Calbo. Prénoms: André. Age: 30. Profession: professeur. Patrie: Zantes. Pièces déposées: passeport. Rue: place St-Gervais. Maison: Aguet. Marié, célibataire ou veuf: Celibat^{re}. Nombre d'enfans: — Observations: Parti pour Lausanne le 4 X^{b} 1824, rendu le pport.* [Under the heading of renewals, arranged in three columns that apparently represent the years 1822, 1823, and 1824, the nine vertical lines indicate the quarterly extensions.] (*Ibid.*, vol. n° 8, année 1822, fol. 265^{v}-266^{r}.)

During the 1822 census, Calvos was registered twice, the house he was living in (Cabrit house, ex-Aguet house) being classified under two different cadastral numbers! I here transcribe (combining the two) the data recorded by the two census-takers:

c/d) *N^{os} des maisons: 153/154. Noms des propriétaires des maisons: Cabrit/(Aguet) Cabri. Noms des individus habitant la maison: Calbro/Calbot. Prénoms: André. Marié, célibataire ou veuf: célibataire/garçon. Lieu d'origine: Italie. Lieu de naissance: Florence. Age: 25. Profession: professeur littérature. Religion: catholique.* (Archives d'Etat de Genève, recensement de 1822, Saint-Gervais, registre F 4, cahiers n°s 17 et 18.)

We can see that Calvos answered the police officer more exactly than the census-takers. Historic truth forces us to recall that he, born in Zante in March 1792, had been baptized according to the Orthodox ritual and that his first marriage, contracted in England, was solemnized on May 18, 1819, according to the Anglican rite.

irreverence are still alive today. Count Capodistria, who happened to be "Genevan" at the same time as Calvos (1822 to 1826), lived in modest dwellings in a patrician residence of the *high town*, on the opposite bank, in the austere shade of St. Peter's cathedral.

We have few precise details about how Calvos spent his time and how he made his living. It seems probable to me that in order to insure his livelihood and to justify his role of professor in the eyes of the authorities, he gave private lessons in Italian and modern Greek, as he had done in London. I suspect that certain Genevan hellenists, eager to know about the state of the language after the classical period and moved by the events of the Greek insurrection to an interest in the descendants of Miltiades and Themistocles, went to Calvos for instruction. But in the present state of my knowledge, I have no proof of what I am putting forward.

We run small risk of being wrong in asserting that Calvos did not renew his public lectures experiment. He gave four lectures in London, in 1818 and 1819, on the relations between modern and ancient Greek. These were favorably received by the *Times* and the *New Times*.[15] Similar lectures given during the first years of the Greek War of Independence would not have passed unnoticed in Geneva, where the newspapers printed everything that concerned Greece from near or far. Yet we have found no such report in the papers of the time, and our feeling is

[15] For reprints of these articles, with Greek translations and comments by C. Th. Dimaras, see "*Γύρω στὸν* Κάλβο *καὶ στὸν* Κοδρικᾶ. *Σχολιασμένα κείμενα*," 'Αγγλοελληνικὴ *ἐπιθεώρηση*, 6 (1953-1954), 250-62.

that Calvos did not swerve from a reserved and studious conduct throughout his sojourn.

In this connection we have some evidence concerning Calvos' personal researches in the public library of Geneva. Bees was the first to call this to the attention of the poet's biographers, and Zoras has recently mentioned it again.[16] Whether through his previous reading or some oral communication by a Genevan scholar, Calvos knew of a precious Greek manuscript of the 13th century containing the text of the *Iliad* with an interlinear prose explanation and scholia. The book had been presented to the Library of Geneva by Daniel Le Clerc in 1702, after having passed through the hands of several eminent scholars, Manuel Moschopoulos among them.[17] Calvos was in no way prepared to study a Renaissance manuscript, but since his early youth he had given striking proof of his thirst for knowledge and capacity for assimilation. Thus, in the library study that was in the old building of the *Collège* founded by Calvin in 1558, he turned himself into a paleographer and a Homerist.

After weeks of study that enabled him to become familiar with the script of the codex and to divine the interest of the Hellenistic and Byzantine commentary, he conceived the idea of editing it and applied to the governors of the library for an authorization to do so. On

[16] N. A. Bees, pp. 19-22; G. Th. Zoras, "'Ο Κάλβος καὶ τὸ ὁμηρικὸν χειρόγραφον τῆς Γενεύης," Παρνασσός, n.s., 11 (1969), 288-96.

[17] J. Nicole, *Les scolies genevoises de l'Iliade publiées avec une étude historique, descriptive et critique sur le Genevensis 44 ou "codex ignotus" d'Henri Estienne et une collation complète de ce manuscrit,* t. I (Paris and London, 1891), pp. ix-xxiv.

September 14, 1822, they dealt with his request, which they examined favorably but refused to grant without a previous opinion from some authority. So the directing council asked Mr. Prevost, one of its members, "to obtain some information concerning the matter from Mr. Coraï in Paris." It seems that the answer of the illustrious philologist was long in coming, or that it was negative; in any case, on January 11, 1823, the governors of the library, examining a new request from Mr. Calbo, did not think it possible to give him a favorable answer. Calvos, whose main fault, I think, had been a desire to take home the priceless manuscript in order to edit it, must have felt bitter indeed about this polite refusal.[18] Whatever the case

[18] The facts are thus reported by Nicole, *ibid.*, pp. xvii-xviii, on the basis of the minutes of the library committee (meetings of September 14, 1822 and January 11, 1823). Nicole's report is reprinted by Bees and Zoras; the latter has published the two extracts from the minutes (Παρνασσός, 11, p. 294, notes 1 and 2). Yet, a third mention escaped the attention of Nicole and the two Greek scholars who used the brilliant study of the Genevan papyrologist. This mention figures in the same manuscript register, in the minutes of the meeting following that of January 11, 1823. I publish this document without comment here, because I intend to come back to this episode later:

Du Samedi 5 Avril 1823

Présens M^rs. Trembley, Masbou, LeFort, Prevost, Pictet, De Candolle, Cellerier, Duby, Picot, Boissier, De la Rive & les 2 Bibliothécaires. . . .

Mr Bourrit rapporte . . . que Mr Weber lui a dit que Mr Senebier faisoit un grand cas de notre manuscrit d'Homère parce qu'il le croyoit unique; mais que lui Mr Weber le juge semblable à celui de St Marc à Venise dont parle d'Anse Villoison parce qu'il a lu les morceaux que cite ce dernier & a trouvé exactement les mêmes dans notre manuscrit, que la paraphrase est bonne, mais que les scholies sont assez mediocres. D'un autre côté M^r. Calbo prétend qu'il y en a un à Londres semblable au nôtre & que ce seroit pour

may be, his preoccupation with Homer, stimulated by the Genevan manuscript, did not remain fruitless; it no doubt contributed to the elaboration of his own language. As proof of this I need only the remarkable Ἐπισημείωσις he added to his first collection of *Odes*, a text in which he formulated, so to speak, his art of poetry. I would be willing to think that the first ten verses of the third book of the *Iliad*, presented there as a specimen of modern heroic verse, were translated by Calvos from the *codex Genavensis Graecus 44*.

I can see another result of the studious hours spent on this manuscript: a letter of thanks addressed, on May 24, 1823, to the first committee of philhellenes of Geneva, in the name of 158 Greeks rescued from the massacres of Moldavia and Wallachia after the defeat of Ypsilanti. These unfortunates crossed into Swiss territory and congregated in Geneva, with the intention of embarking eventually at Marseilles for the return to their country. The document, which was published only recently on the occasion of the centenary of the death of Jean-Gabriel Eynard,[19] consists of an address in calligraphic script followed by the autograph signatures transliterated into French, with a mention of the place of origin of each signer. Indications concerning the illiterate are recorded in French. In our

---

*prévenir l'édition de Londres qu'il voudroit imprimer le nôtre. La Direction ne se croit pas assez éclairée pour juger de l'importance du manuscrit, mais comme M*r. *Calbo n'a pas réitéré la demande de l'avoir on ajourne toute décision à cet égard.*

(Genève, Bibliothèque publique et universitaire, Archives H 2, "Registre des Assemblées de Messieurs les Directeurs de la Bibliothèque pour les années 1734 & suiv^{tes}," fol. 184^{v}-185^{r}).

[19] M. Bouvier-Bron, *Jean-Gabriel Eynard (1775-1863) et le philhellénisme genevois*, Geneva, 1963, pp. 15-16 and facsimile.

opinion both the Greek text of the address and the French transcriptions are in Calvos' own hand. The letter of thanks, written in archaic Greek, deserves our full attention here (*fig.* 1):

> *Ἐξ ἀρχῆς μὲν τοῦ παρόντος ἔτους καὶ ἕως τὴν σήμερον ἡμέραν τῶν εἰς τὴν ἐπιούσιον τροφὴν χρημάτων ἀποροῦντες, καὶ παρὰ τοῖς γενναίοις Ἑλβετοῖς φιλανθρώπως φιλοξενηθέντες· πάλιν δὲ ἐξ ὅτου ἐπιστρέψαι εἰς τὴν φίλην ἡμῶν πατρίδα οὐκ ἔχοντες, καὶ παρ' αὐτοῖς τὰ ἀναγκαῖα πορισθέντες· ἡμεῖς οἱ ὑπογεγραμμένοι Ἕλληνες χάριν διὰ τοῦ γράμματος τούτου τοῖς ἡμᾶς εὐεργετήσασιν ἀποδίδομεν, καὶ εὐχόμεθα τῷ παντοδυνάμῳ θεῷ παρέχειν αὐτοῖς ἀπόλαυσιν εὐτυχίας τε καὶ εἰρήνης, εὐπορίαν παντὸς ἀγαθοῦ, αἰώνιον μὲν ἐλευθερίαν, ἀγήρατον ὁμόνοιαν, στεφάνους δὲ ἀρετῆς, δῶρα δὲ ἀμάραντα πολυχρύσων τεχνῶν τε καὶ ἐπιστημῶν, καὶ οὐράνιον βοήθειαν.*
>
> Ἐν Γενεύῃ, τῇ κδ' Μαΐου, ᾳωκγ'.[20]

In translation:

From the beginning of the year unto this day, deprived of the money indispensable for our daily sustenance, we have been most hospitably sheltered by the generous Helvetians; devoid of the means to return to our be-

[20] The original contains the wrong spellings *γενναῖοις*, *φιλοξενιθέντες*, *τοῦτου*, *Γενέβῃ*. In spite of the stylized penmanship and the studied archaism of the writing, one will recognize Calvos' "Greek hand" in a close comparison of our document with the facsimiles of the ode to Napoleon published by Vitti, *Kalvos e i suoi scritti in italiano*, last plate and Νέα Ἑστία, Vol. 72, p. 1,085. Concerning his "French hand" (lower part of the Genevan document), it is obviously identical with the "Italian hand" of the Bologna and Vatican manuscripts (Vitti, *Kalvos*, pl. I-V).

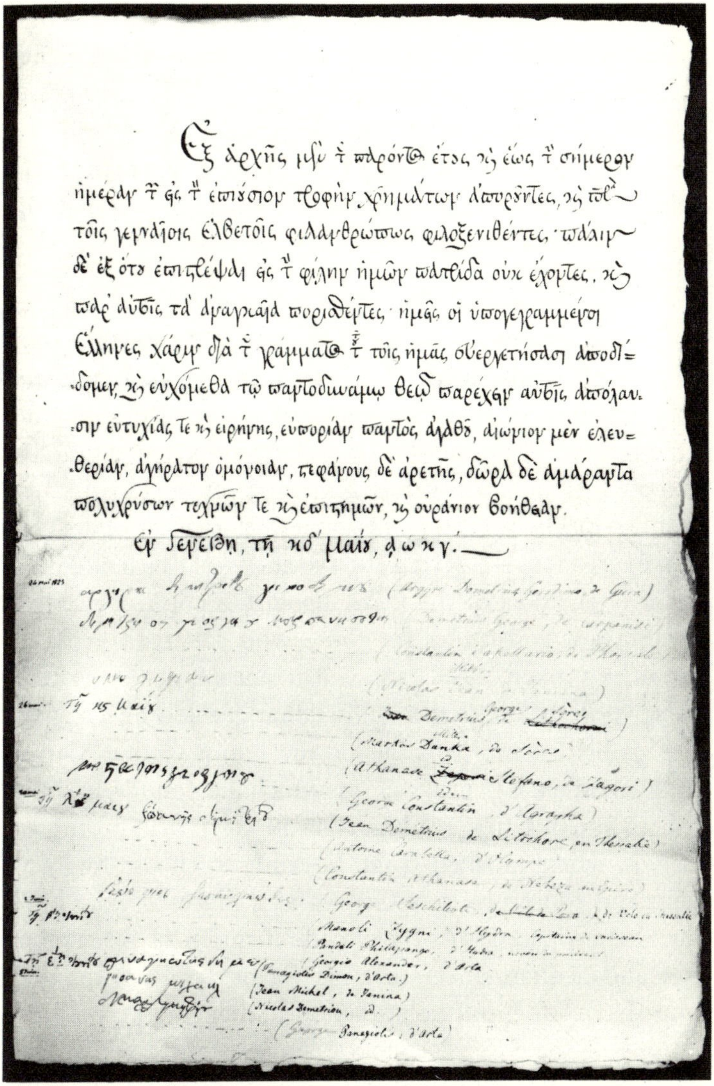

Ἐξ ἀρχῆς μὲν τοῦ παρόντος ἔτους καὶ ἕως τῆς σήμερον ἡμέρας τῆς εἰς τὴν ἐπιούσιον τροφὴν χρημάτων ἀποροῦντες, καὶ παρὰ τοῖς γενναίοις Ἑλβετοῖς φιλανθρώπως φιλοξενηθέντες· πάλιν δὲ ἐξ ὅτου ἐπιστρέψαι εἰς τὴν φίλην ἡμῶν πατρίδα οὐκ ἔχοντες, καὶ παρ' αὐτοῖς τὰ ἀναγκαῖα πορισθέντες· ἡμᾶς οἱ ὑπογεγραμμένοι Ἕλληνες χάριν διὰ τοῦ γράμματος τούτου τοῖς ἡμᾶς εὐεργετήσασι ἀποδίδομεν, καὶ εὐχόμεθα τῷ παντοδυνάμῳ θεῷ παρέχειν αὐτοῖς ἀπόλαυσιν εὐτυχίας τε καὶ εἰρήνης, εὐπορίαν παντὸς ἀγαθοῦ, αἰώνιον μὲν ἐλευθερίαν, ἀκήρατον ὁμόνοιαν, στεφάνους δὲ ἀρετῆς, δῶρα δὲ ἀμάραντα πολυχρύσων τεχνῶν τε καὶ ἐπιστημῶν, καὶ οὐράνιον βοήθειαν.

Ἐν Γενεύῃ, τῇ κδ' Μαΐου, αωκγ'.

fig. 1 *Letter of thanks to the Genevan philhellenes, May 24, 1823 (Calvos' autograph). Geneva, Bibliothèque publique et universitaire, Ms. suppl. 1885, fol.* 88r.

loved country, we have been furnished by them with all that was necessary; so we, the undersigned Hellenes, bear witness by this letter to our gratitude to our benefactors, and pray to Almighty God that He may grant them enjoyment of felicity and peace, abundance of every good, eternal liberty, everlasting harmony, the laurels of virtue, the imperishable gifts of rich-yielding arts and sciences, and the help of heaven. Geneva, May 24th, 1823.

This document has a threefold interest. From the point of view of handwriting, it appears, through ligatures and abbreviations, so unusual compared to the Greek of that time that we may consider it an exercise in paleography, executed under the direct influence of a Renaissance manuscript. From the point of view of style, it offers certain expressions—especially at the end—that bear the hallmark of the poet of the *Odes*. From the point of view of meaning, it constitutes for those who can read between the lines a token, as elegant as it is sincere, of the writer's personal gratitude to the country that granted him refuge.

This brings me to speak of the "milieu" that Calvos frequented in Geneva, one in which he found his publishers and his first readers. The motives that prompted Calvos, when expelled from Tuscany, to choose Switzerland and more precisely Geneva as a place of exile have puzzled people. Critics have made mention of the memories and acquaintances that his former passage in 1816 must have left him, the attraction he felt for the political regime of the Swiss Republics, and especially the ardent philhellenic movement that had manifested itself everywhere in Switzerland, in all classes of society, after the outbreak of the War of Independence.[21] All this is not wrong, but it pertains to an idealized view of things, and requires that distinctions be made. Five years previously, in Zurich, in the company of Foscolo, Calvos had suffered bitterly from isolation, increased no doubt by the language barrier; he had tested the limits of Swiss neutrality and had felt the hold the powers of the Holy Alliance still exercised on the governments of a confederation that they had declared independent and sovereign by the treaties of 1814. The very fact that Calvos chose for his second sojourn a canton of French-speaking Switzerland, and more particularly the Republic of Geneva (the latest to join the Swiss Confederation), seems to me to indicate how little he wished to renew his impressions of 1816.

Concerning the philhellenic movement, we must remember that it spread like a tidal wave from north to south, and that, starting from the liberal areas of Germany, it very swiftly reached German Switzerland, but less so French Switzerland. In April 1821, it was not primarily as a Greek, child of a race that had just started its struggle against its age-old oppressor, that Calvos came to Geneva, but as an Italian exile, member of an organization that was preparing the peninsula's uprising against its Austrian occupier. He knew that in Geneva, as in London,[22] he would find Italian patriots who were animated by the same ideal, who would help him to live. Because of its geographical situation at the confines of the Kingdom of Sardinia, Geneva had in effect become the

[21] See Bees, p. 7.

[22] Vitti, *Πηγὲς γιὰ τὴ βιογραφία τοῦ Κάλβου*, especially the letters of Bartolomeo De Sanctis, nos. 43-61, pp. 42-49 and notes pp. 142-43.

rallying point of the Carbonari, grouped around the famous Buonarroti.[23] This is the main reason that brought the banished Calvos to this city. Though I have not examined the entire vast documentation, both manuscript and printed, concerning the subject, I still put forth this hypothesis; and I do not think later research will disprove it.

Among the meeting places of the Italian refugees were the reception rooms and the library of the Société de Lecture. I must say a few words about this institution, which honors my city and which expresses perfectly the "esprit de Genève" in the first half of the 19th century.[24] It was founded in 1816 by a group of enlightened citizens, among whom we may mention a botanist of world-wide reputation (de Candolle), the financier of genius who became the life and soul of European philhellenism (Eynard), and a figure of some learning, a man-of-the-world who was to preside over the first "society for the emancipation of the Greeks" (Favre-Bertrand). The Geneva Reading Society had a quick development and enjoyed a renown that reached beyond our borders. Its collections consisted of books donated by new members and of purchases that covered all fields of human knowledge. To the books were added newspapers and periodicals from various countries —they numbered 92 in 1820—that enabled the public, admitted almost without formalities, to keep informed of scientific, political, and literary news. Established in the elegant mansion that the Resident of France had inhab-

[23] G. Ferretti, *Esuli del Risorgimento in Svizzera*, Bologna, 1948, pp. 97-137.

[24] Fr. De Crue, *Genève et la Société de Lecture* (1816-1896), Geneva, 1896, particularly pp. 51-76.

ited, the Société de Lecture very early became a meeting place and a salon for conversation. One could meet there members of the local aristocracy, professors of the Academy, and students and foreigners, both noble and plebeian, who lived in Geneva or were only passing through it.

A little inquiry into the archives of the Société de Lecture yields the fact that Monsieur André Calbo obtained his membership card probably in 1822, under the presidency of the eminent jurist and publicist Étienne Dumont, formerly secretary to Mirabeau. In 1824, Calvos volunteered to translate the Greek papers received by the society. In the president's report of January 20, 1825, he appeared on the list of donors for the previous year, together with Julien of Paris.[25] This is not a usurped title, since we can find at the Société de Lecture, under the call number 12968, the collection *La Lyre*, containing the first ten odes of Andreas Calvos, bound together with their French translation by Stanislas Julien.

Before examining this copy of the original edition more closely, let us speak of a few people whom Calvos may have met in this privileged place, halfway between his lodgings at St. Gervais and the Academy library. His contemporary Jean Humbert (1792-1851) was probably his sponsor, as well as that of so many other Greeks he introduced into the Reading Society. Though he was a good hellenist and a declared philhellene, he nevertheless devoted his main efforts to oriental studies. Author of an *Arabic Anthology* published in 1819, which exercised unquestioned influence upon the French romantics, he held the chair of Arabic literature and language that the Acad-

[25] Société de Lecture de Genève, annual reports (manuscript register), report of Prof. P.-F. Bellot, January 20, 1825, p. 5.

emy of Geneva created for him. In the question of contemporary literature he had, as a friend of Lamartine, taken the side of the moderns against classicism.[26] It was he who, a year and a half after Calvos' departure, invited the Phanariot diplomat and man of letters Iakovakis Rizos Neroulos to Geneva, and urged him to teach a course in modern Greek literature. Humbert prepared the lectures from this course for publication in 1827.[27] He probably introduced his students of ancient Greek to Calvos, especially the most gifted among them, young Élie-Ami Bétant (1803-1871). Destined to an honorable career as hellenist and pedagogue, Bétant had an experience, from 1827 to 1828, that was to mark him for life: he was engaged by John Capodistria in the capacity of secretary, and he lived exciting and exhausting months by the side of the first president of the young Greek state. Since his university years, Bétant had been interested in modern Greece and in its language; and it is very possible that he received lessons from Calvos. In return, this meticulous man, who was later to compose a justly appreciated *Lexicon Thucydideum* and to initiate forty classes of high school students into the morphology and syntax of classical Greek—this man may have helped the poet of the *Odes* to draw up his glossary. The curious Πίναξ λέξεων καὶ φράσεων that was published as an appendix to the poems was obviously

[26] On J. Humbert, see A. Louca, "Catalogue des manuscrits arabes. Bibliothèque publique et universitaire de Genève," periodical *Genava*, 16 (1968), 6-7, and "Arabisants de Genève," *Musées de Genève*, 91 (1969), 5-6.

[27] Cours de littérature grecque moderne, donné à Genève par Jacovaky Rizo Néroulos, . . . publié par Jean Humbert, Geneva and Paris, 1827; second edition, revised and enlarged, Geneva and Paris, 1828.

directed toward foreign readers who had a classical training and who were eager to confront with their school memories the literary production of a Greek living in their own day.[28]

Calvos' relationship with a third personage whom he met at the Société de Lecture is less subject to hypothesis. This person was Charles Didier, a poet, traveler, journalist, and novelist who started his career in Geneva, his native city, but who later went to try his luck in Paris. There he lived in the shadow of Victor Hugo, George Sand, and Charles Nodier, and there he died in 1864: poor, forgotten by his countrymen, and without having achieved fame.[29] We have several indications of the friendship that bound Calvos and Didier, whose temperaments must have served to bring the two together and whose destinies show some resemblance. I shall only mention one detail (it may seem slight at first glance, but it is a telling one): the autograph manuscript of the first ten odes, which is full of corrections by the author and which served as the text for the original printing (Geneva, 1824), is now in the Sainte-Geneviève Library in Paris.[30] On the first page it

[28] On Bétant's life and work, see my study "Élie-Ami Bétant (1803-1871), régent et principal du Collège, philhellène, helléniste et citoyen," *Le Collège de Genève, 1559-1959. Mélanges historiques et littéraires* (Geneva, 1959), pp. 109-30. A reprint of Calvos' glossary, with preliminary remarks by G. Th. Zoras, appeared in *Νέα Ἑστία*, 68 (1960), 1,081-1,086.

[29] J. Sellards, *Dans le sillage du romantisme. Charles Didier (1805-1864)*, Paris, 1933.

[30] Pointed out in 1917 by G. Dossios. The manuscript has been examined by H. Pernot (Études de littérature grecque moderne, 2e série, Paris, 1918, pp. 129-30). D. Zakythinos made a first collation of it ("*Ἕνα χειρόγραφο τῶν ᾠδῶν τοῦ Κάλβου*," *Ἡμερολόγιον τῆς Μεγάλης Ἑλλάδος* [Athens, 1930], pp. 307-12) and more recently

bears the simple inscription: "C. Didier. Don de l'auteur," and underneath it, two annotations in another hand which indicate that Ch. Em. Ruelle received the manuscript from M. A. Aubry, bookseller, in January 1865, and that he donated it to the Bibliothèque Sainte-Geneviève in January 1883. This means, if I am correct, that as soon as the *Lyre* came off the press, Calvos entrusted the original manuscript to his friend Didier, and that Didier kept it reverently until his death. A Paris bookseller bought it the next year, no doubt together with other papers left by the Genevan poet, and offered it to Ruelle, who in turn donated it to the Sainte-Geneviève Library.

We must, before closing, have a look at the little book that constitutes the outcome of Calvos' Genevan years. The original edition of the *Lyre* is extremely rare today; it is very highly esteemed by book-lovers for its careful printing, equal indeed to the best productions of the workshop of Jules-Guillaume Fick, the inheritor of a tradition that goes back to the great printer and humanist Robert Estienne.[31] To my knowledge, there are four copies of the book in Geneva. The Public and University Library possesses three, of which two came from donations made in 1838 and 1900, and the third from a purchase made in the 1920's.[32] These three copies are in a perfect state of preservation and free from old annotations.

F. M. Pontani ("Per un' edizione critica di Kalvos," *Helikon*, 4 [Messina, 1964], 83-94) has submitted it to a close study in connection with his critical edition.

[31] A. Cartier, "L'imprimerie Fick," *Nos anciens et leurs œuvres*, Geneva, 1901, p. 41 ff.

[32] Bibliothèque publique et universitaire, call numbers Hga 900, Hga 943, and S 19244.

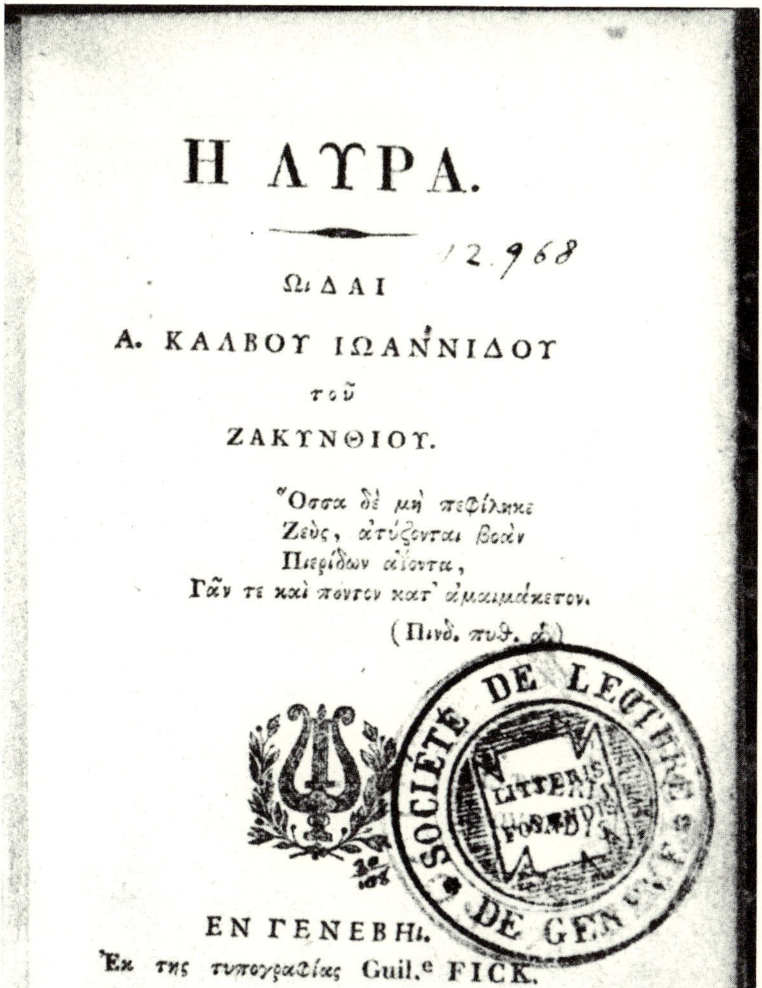

Η ΛΥΡΑ.

12.968

ΩιΔΑΙ

Α. ΚΑΛΒΟΥ ΙΩΑΝΝΙΔΟΥ

τοῦ

ΖΑΚΥΝΘΙΟΥ.

Ὅσσα δὲ μὴ πεφίληκε
Ζεὺς, ἀτύζονται βοὰν
Πιερίδων ἀΐοντα,
Γᾶν τε καὶ πόντον κατ᾽ ἀμαιμάκετον.
(Πινδ. πυθ. α.)

EN ΓΕΝΕΒΗι.
Ἐκ τῆς τυπογραφίας Guil.e FICK.

ΑιΩΚΔ.

fig. 2 Greek title-page of the Lyre, *Geneva 1824, copy presented by the poet to the Geneva Reading Society.*

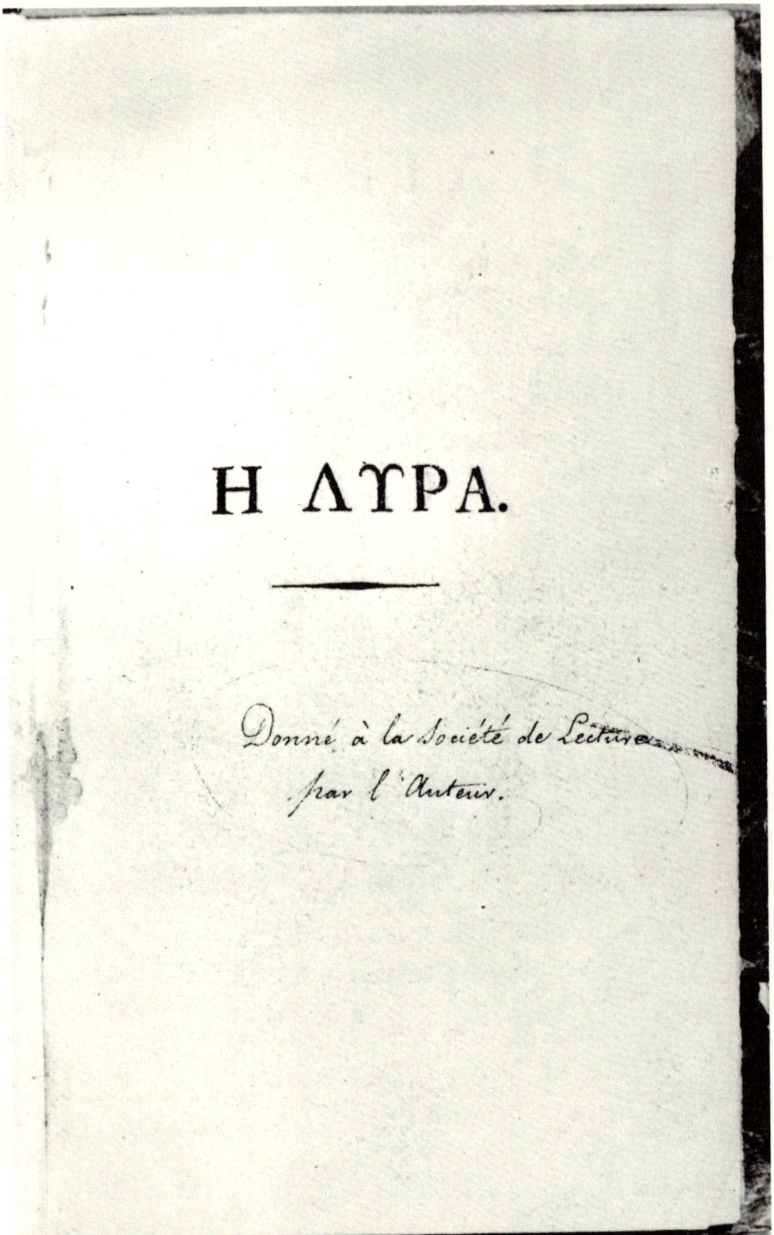

fig. 3 Half-title of the Lyre, *with Calvos' dedication to the Société de Lecture.*

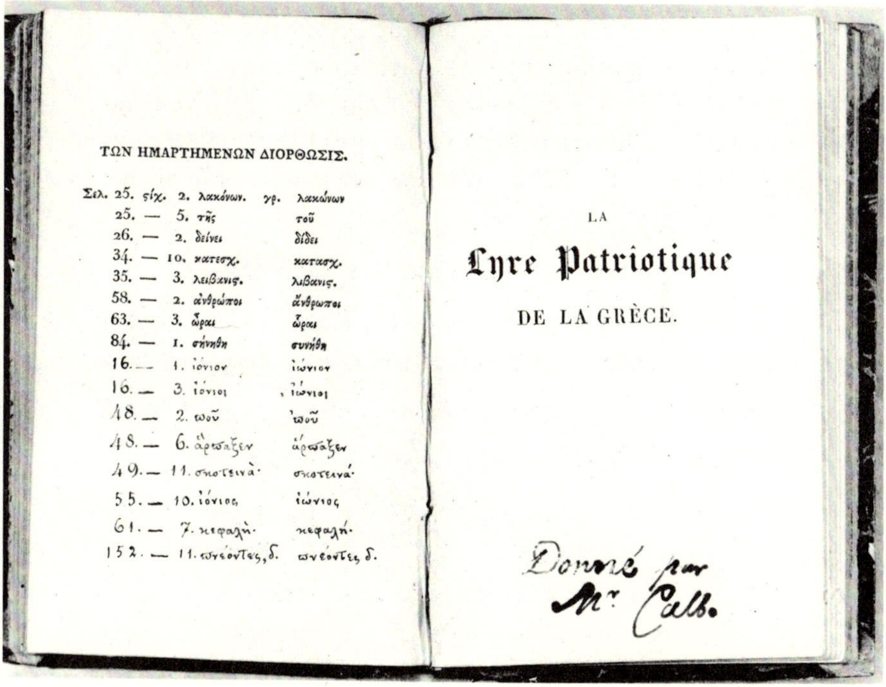

fig. 4

(a) *Last page of the* Lyre, *printed errata with autograph additions. Copy of the Geneva Reading Society.*

(b) *Half-title of the French translation of the* Lyre, *Paris 1824, with Calvos' inscription to the Société de Lecture.*

The fourth copy is that of the Société de Lecture, which the organizers of the MGSA Princeton Symposium can claim to have brought back to light (*fig.* 2).[33] Some autograph additions make it a unique specimen:

1. On the half-title (*fig.* 3), the author has inscribed the copy to the Society in the same elegant and sensitive hand in which we have seen (above, in *fig.* 1) the names transliterated into French in the address to the philhellenic committee:

Donné à la Société de Lecture par l'Auteur.

2. On the last page, the following eight lines are added to the errata in careful imitation of the preceding type (*fig.* 4a):

[*page*		*line*	*instead of*	*read*]
16.	—	1.	*ἰόνιον*	*ἰώνιον*
16.	—	3.	*ἰόνιοι*	*ἰώνιοι*
48.	—	2.	*ποῦ*	*'ποῦ*
48.	—	6.	*ἃρπαξεν*	*ἅρπαξεν*
49.	—	11.	*σκοτεινὰ·*	*σκοτεινά·*
55.	—	10.	*ἰόνιος*	*ἰώνιος*
61.	—	7.	*κεφαλὴ·*	*κεφαλή·*
152.	—	11.	*πνέοντες, δ.*	*πνέοντες δ.*[34]

3. On the half-title of the French translation (which is bound together with the original Greek collection, as al-

[33] This essay was originally prepared for delivery at the symposium in 1969.

[34] This addendum to the errata slip presents nothing extraordinary, but it is at least proof of the scrupulous care with which Calvos revised the edition and of his obstinate preference for the erroneous form ἰώνιος (on this point, see Pontani, *op.cit.*, p. 85).

ready noted) we find the author's inscription once more, but in a thicker pen (*fig.* 4b):

Donné par Mr. Calbo

These are the elements I have intended to present regarding Calvos in Geneva. I hope that, in spite of their fragmentary and sometimes conjectural character, they will shed some light on the circumstances that, in the liberal Geneva of 1824, urged a child of the Ionian islands, nourished by the literary traditions of Italy and raised in the struggles of his time, to become a Greek poet.[35]

[35] Since this paper was sent to the editors (January 1970), valuable contributions have enriched Calvian bibliography. Special mention is due to the careful, diplomatic edition of the twenty *Odes* by F. M. Pontani (Ἀνδρέα Κάλβου Ὠδαί, *κριτικὴ ἔκδοση*, ed. Filippo Maria Pontani, *εἰσαγωγὴ* Κ. Θ. Δημαρᾶς, *γλωσσάριο* Anna Gentilini, Athens, 1970). Complementary research has been done by G. Th. Zoras (Νέα Καλβικά, Athens, 1970) and interesting material, especially iconographic, has been published by K. H. Metaxas ("Andrea Kalvo Centenary," *The Greek Gazette*, vol. 4, no. 36, London, August 1970).

Angelos Terzakis

3. *Matesis'* VASSILIKOS: *The First Drama of Ideas*

THE FOCUS of this essay will be a dramatic work, a play that was precocious for the Greek literature of its time and prophetic for European literature in general. I should immediately say that I shall try not to exaggerate in order to prove the validity of my point. As I hope my readers will realize, the play in question does not need any underlining. What is needed is that the barrier that keeps it from international attention be overcome, since modern Greek is read by only a few outside Greece.

My intention is to look at the play from an artistic-esthetic point of view and to throw some light upon its ideological climate and the intellectual messages that inform it. Representative as these messages are of the time the play was written, they also connect it with the wider European thought and tradition of the beginnings of the 19th century, and this adds to its artistic significance an importance that is social and moral.

The play is *Vassilikos* (The Basil Plant) by Andonis Matesis. It was written in Zante between 1829 and 1830. Zante, together with the other Ionian Islands, was at that time a British protectorate, having been dominated previously by the French and before that by the Venetians. The mainland of Greece had just been liberated from Turkish rule by the War of Independence of 1821, one of the most liberal and heroic movements in modern history.

During the years when Matesis was writing *Vassilikos* there was considerable cultural inequality between the mainland of Greece and the Ionian Islands living under Western rule. While on the mainland smoke was still rising from the guns of the War of Independence, the Ionian Islands were in direct contact with Southwestern and Central Europe and its intellectual climate. Those of the educated islanders who had not studied abroad, had read, in any case, foreign literary works in the original Italian, French, English, or German. Especially in Zante an intellectual coterie had been formed around the poet Dionysios Solomos, who, for his long poem "Hymn to Liberty" (1823)—which was inspired by the War of Independence—as well as for the rest of his poetry, was recognized as the national poet and the island's intellectual leader. Andonis Matesis, the author of *Vassilikos*, was only four years Solomos' junior and was part of his coterie. The general line of this school, later to be called "Heptanesian," was that it based its artistic and ideological creed upon the spoken language of the people, the *demotic*, which was to become the language of modern Greek literature.

This was in general the literary background of the work. But when we speak specifically about a dramatic work, a play, other questions naturally arise. Was there any theatre—as an organized artistic activity, an established institution—where this play was born? The answer is no. Theatre, as we understand it today, and as it was understood in the rest of Europe, did not exist in the Zante of 1830. I mean that it did not exist as a professional institution; it did exist in an elementary stage, in the form of open-air shows set up in the streets of the town and performed by amateurs. These shows, called *homilies*, were for the most part improvisations full of rough humor. They amply testified, however, to the natural inclination of an instinctively art-loving people toward theatrical expression.

In 1795, thirty years before the appearance of *Vassilikos*, another intellectual from Zante, Demetrios Gouzelis, had written a comedy in which the hero was the internationally established stereotype of the braggart. If one were to go further back, he would detect in those early plays of the Ionian theatre the influence of a really great moment: that of the theatre which had flourished in Crete in the 17th century. When Crete was taken by the Turks in 1669, the numerous refugees went to the Ionian Islands, carrying manuscripts, memoirs, and an oral theatrical tradition with them. Thus, starting from the 17th century and coming to the beginnings of the 18th, we can establish the cultural and national genealogy that will explain *Vassilikos* from a historical point of view.

But historical explanation is not always an explanation in depth. To get closer to our objective, we need some more specific information and comparisons. Those who can read *Vassilikos* in the original, in the idiomatic and picturesque language of its time and place, will be strongly impressed by one thing: the highly individual character of the play.

First of all, the play is endowed with a technique unexpected in an inexperienced playwright. Its structure is perfect, its action tightly knit, its progression steadily rising, its characters drawn in relief, its atmosphere fully authentic and radiating from the core of the drama. Second, *Vassilikos* is a social and ideological drama written at a time when its genre had not yet reached its apex in Western Europe. One of our scholars thought that he recognized in *Vassilikos* the influence of Schiller, especially of his play *Kabale und Liebe* (*Love and Intrigue* or *Louise Miller*). I disagree. The two plays have nothing in common. Schiller's is a bourgeois drama from the point of view of its heroine and her family. Matesis' play deals with the aristocracy. There is no analogy between the two plots and their development. Schiller's play has a sad ending while Matesis' has a happy one. Only one character, and that secondary, seems to be their single point of analogy: Wurm of *Kabale und Liebe* has some psychological affinities with Gherassimakis of *Vassilikos*; but both of them are no more than personal variations on the widely established prototype of the villain. In addition, while the villain in Schiller's melodrama is quite conventional, Matesis produced a villain who is highly real. There is no question that Matesis had studied Schiller; but studying does not necessarily mean imitating: it means learning. It is quite obvious that the Greek playwright had found the prototype for Gherassimakis in the life around him; otherwise he would not have been able to give him such authenticity.

If we wish to find the right place for *Vassilikos* in its time, there is another comparison, by far more enlightening, that we should take into account. The year 1830—the year the play is dated—stands as a landmark in the history of European theatre. In that year the French romantic school made its theatrical debut with Victor Hugo's *Hernani*, and that landmark has since been called the year of the "battle of Hernani."

If we compare *Hernani* with *Vassilikos*, we are bound to discover something unexpected: that *Hernani* is a poor play written in excellent verse. Melodrama, pompous inspiration, rhetoric, boastfulness, improbabilities—not out of faulty imagination but out of naïveté—are its characteristics throughout. It is not only by chance that, outside France, the play was pushed aside by Verdi's opera of the same title. In contrast, *Vassilikos* is a vital picture of a time and its problems: no boastfulness and no magniloquence.

Everything is expressed simply, warmly, and with the immediacy of truth.

I do not intend by this either to underestimate Victor Hugo or to overestimate Matesis unduly; I only wish to show how literary history is made at times. Under different circumstances, *Vassilikos* would have been considered *the* theatrical accomplishment of 1830. Human circumstance, not always based on justice, determined that the year in question be called the *Hernani* year. It is the lucky ones who make literary history.

But to get closer to my theme, let me turn to a résumé of the play itself (which is unfortunately not available in English translation), after a few remarks on the context in which it was shaped. The author does not place the action of *Vassilikos* in his own time. He goes back one hundred and twenty years, and he has his reasons for doing so. In 1712 the Ionian Islands were under Venetian domination. The Very Serene Democracy of St. Mark, successor to the Franks in that part of the Mediterranean, had introduced into those islands the social system functioning in its own domain, the feudal system. At the top was the nobility, registered in the *libro d'oro*; at the bottom were the people, the *popolari*, professionals, small businessmen, craftsmen, farmers, and serfs. There was also a middle class, the bourgeoisie. But the nobility was so closed, so inflexible about its hierarchy among men and the safeguarding of its privileges, that further distinctions existed even within the ranks of the upper class itself. The first grade of nobility could not think of becoming connected, through marriage, with the second. It should be noted that in 1712 Louis XIV was still King of France, and this is a very meaningful historical fact. We are still far from the subsequent liberalism of the 18th century, later to be called the Age of Enlightenment.

Another important fact is that the author of *Vassilikos* belonged to the aristocracy. His play, therefore, is not an outburst of envy or social hatred but the product of an enlightened awareness and an artistically accomplished ideological criticism. Andonis Matesis, the aristocrat, was intellectually part of his time in the sense that he breathed in its refreshing avant-garde breezes. With his *Vassilikos* he accomplished a well-balanced leap in history by projecting the revolutionary, progressive ideas of his own day into a world considerably older. He did this in order to produce dramatic vitality. In 1712 the feudal system was still at its peak, and its foundations had not yet started cracking. There was only one sign prophetic of what was to come: in 1628 the first social uprising took place in Zante, what was known as the "rebellion of the popolari." The occasion was drowned in blood, but it is significant that one hundred and sixty-one years before the French Revolution the socially oppressed people in the Ionian Islands rose up against tyranny. We can notice again how badly, how unfairly, history is written. In 1628, the year of that uprising, Louis XIII reigned in France, with Cardinal Richelieu as his right hand. The French still had to bear another two Louis before the Revolution.

Now to the play. It is divided into five acts, in keeping with neoclassical standards. Its protagonist, the nobleman Darios Ronkalas, is at the height of his prosperity, rich in estates, and in his way tyrannical and oppressive. Cruel by nature, strongly adhering to the omnipotence of the *pater familias*, he has one ideal: to safeguard the economic foundation of his household and to keep its honor unsullied. The Greek word for honor, *timi*, also means price or value. In the mind of Ronkalas, it carries this second economic connotation as well.

Ronkalas tells his son, Draghanighos, a young man who happens to be inspired by the progressive and humanistic ideas of a time that was to come much later: "In the case of families with the misfortune of having many females born into them, would you wish the family's fortune dissipated from one generation to the next by being given away as dowries? Is this what you in your wisdom consider reasonable? We should not, in order to please a woman who appears for a little while in the world and then disappears, do harm to the family fortune which stays forever and remains known."

This is not niggardliness. Ronkalas voices the mystic belief in the sacredness of the family and in the superiority of his class. For this same reason—family-and-class pride—he does not want to see his only daughter, Gharoufalia, married, not even at the cost of a small dowry. "None of the females in our family ever took a small dowry," he argues. So neither large nor small dowry is to be given her. All that is left for poor Gharoufalia is for her to be sacrificed; her father decides to send her to a nunnery. He hopes she will become a mother superior because this, according to the views of the time, would enhance the prestige of the family.

But Darios' decision, without his suspecting it, is taken too late. The young noblewoman, during the carnival season, loses her way in a sudden downpour. Searching for shelter, she ventures into a lonely and deserted hut, where she is seduced by a drunken young man. When the play begins, Gharoufalia is already pregnant. Fortunately, her lover is not a scoundrel but a young nobleman of the second class of nobility. He regrets his deed, and is willing to right his wrong. Gharoufalia, for her part, has fallen in love with him. But there is now an insuperable obstacle standing between them: Darios, with furious indignation, drives away the mediators that the young lover, Filippakis, sends to him. A Ronkalas will never give his daughter in marriage to an inferior, the offspring of a family less illustrious than his own. In addition, marriage would mean that he would have to give her a dowry.

This is not, however, the main conflict in the play; the real conflict is on a level more ideological than sentimental. It is the conflict between father and son—between Darios, who does not know of his daughter's error, and Draghanighos, who does know of it but who has forgiven his sister and stands on her side, full of affection, humanity, and understanding. The conflict, in other words, is between one who represents an obsolete status ossified in the midst of its prejudices, and one who speaks for a world that is to come. The crisis, therefore, is historical, and the conflict critical.

Another virtue of *Vassilikos* is to the point here. Its central characters are not merely bearers of views and ideas, mouthpieces in a theoretical dispute; the play does not have the moral frigidity and the outdated dogmatism of the ideological theatre that was to flourish in Europe later on. The conflict in *Vassilikos* is between father and son, not between the party chief of feudalism and the party chief of rebellion. The end is a happy one because the old world is already condemned to die. Ronkalas, carried away by the moralism of his time, appoints a confederate to shoot at the man who boasted of planning to climb up at night to steal a pot of basil from Gharoufalia's windowsill. Basil thus becomes a major symbol in the play. He who dared to do the act, however, was not Filippakis, as Ronkalas thought, but a drunken *popolaros*, an unfortunate poor lover, who does it for the sake of his own beloved, a certain girl named Vassilo.

Ronkalas is now in danger of being irreparably exposed as the instigator of the killing of an innocent man. Draghanighos is the one who saves the situation. Gharoufalia, hearing that her lover was presumed to have been shot and perhaps killed, faints. The big secret now escapes from her mother's mouth. Out of his mind, Ronkalas draws a knife to kill both his wife and daughter, but is disarmed by his son after a short fight. Facing the alternative of either ruining his reputation by being exposed as the instigator of murder or of suffering his daughter's marriage, Ronkalas, humiliated now, is forced to yield and accept the lesser of the two evils: the marriage.

The dramatic progress of the plot is very skillfully handled. Nothing appears forced or concocted by the author; nothing happens outside a logical sequence or without psychological necessity. The play is, however, a long one: half again as long as a normal play. Fortunately it can be cut without loss to its substance, and it is usually performed in Greece in a shortened version. It seems that Matesis wanted it to be effective for reading as well as staging. In his prologue he calls it "a historical novel dramatically presented," then goes on immediately to explain the dramatic rules that he followed. By "historical novel" he means a portrait of the character and the customs of that time: the beginning of the 18th century.

The play opens with a very skillfully constructed exposition, enacted by Filippakis in his anxiety as he stands under Gharoufalia's window. Something out of Beaumarchais' *Barber of Seville* seems to have entered this idyllic street-scene, yet probably without any direct influence from the French playwright. The wages that Filippakis owes Ghlossidis, his servant, reminds one of a similar situation in Molière, and even earlier, in the *Commedia dell' Arte*, with its youthful and prodigal lovers, whom we also find in Goldoni.

Matesis provides also for the dramatic presentation of incidental street movement in the staging of the play. The various peddlers and hawkers, each one with his singular and melodic cry, weave their way through the picturesque atmosphere of an island street so as to make it truly Mediterranean and Greek. In the third act, which also takes place in the street at night, we hear the famous serenades of Zante sung under the young nobleman's window. Here again, we detect Matesis' genuine theatrical instinct. At every phrase in the play the reader or spectator feels like exclaiming: "What a wonderful gift for theatre." Characterization in particular seems to be the work of a master craftsman (although Matesis was actually the author of only one play).

There are also certain moments in *Vassilikos* of unexpected succinctness and compactness, moments of a pure theatrical rhetoric—the conclusion of Act Two, for instance, when Gharoufalia in a critical moment orders her maid Lanaro to take in the pot of basil as the night falls, and Lanaro, out of laziness, leaves it there on the windowsill. This episode takes on a double significance: on the one hand, it brings back to our minds the "basil" theme with an indirect and rather *sotto voce* tragicality; on the other hand, it prepares for the play's climax. How wonderfully the playwright builds to the climax, when, in the last act, the frightened and distraught mother reveals to the speechless father Gharoufalia's condition! The conclusion of the play has an exemplary compactness, an anti-melodramatic eloquence, an almost modern brevity. Draghanighos has sent for Filippakis. The whole family is on stage. Ronkalas, powerless now, rages in anger. Suddenly Lanaro is heard announcing that the bridegroom-to-be has arrived. Ronkalas goes through a last convulsive writhing. Gharoufalia feels her knees yielding; she is ready to faint. Draghanighos holds her up and takes her across the room to face the drawing-room door. Filippakis enters. "Gharoufalia!" he cries, and she responds: "Is that you, Filippakis?" The curtain falls.

The depiction of customs and manners in *Vassilikos* is abundant, but the main stress in the play is on the human drama: the characters in their social and psychological situation. The figure of Darios Ronkalas stands towering in the center of the picture. He is a strong man, with patriarchal principles, the scion of a race with a long tradition behind it. His family originated in Venice and has since gone through generations of hellenization. Gherasimakis, the wicked man in the play, at one point calls Ronkalas a "ghost" (*vrykolakas*), and this characterization is a real discovery. He is not, however, the ghost of someone long dead, but that of a past time full of violence and blood, a past which insists on living still. The play marks a critical reversal, the moment when the historical balance is tipped. Ronkalas sees his son Draghanighos, whom he looks upon with contempt and considers the black sheep of his family, now grasp his arm powerfully and render him helpless. At the moment when Ronkalas is disarmed, a whole world collapses.

To the social difference between the families of Ronkalas and Ghiaghyropoulos, of the father-in-law and the son-in-law-to-be, a family hatred is added. The reader of *Vassilikos* may at this point think of *Romeo and Juliet*, although the affinity between the two plays is limited to this external element. In a deeper sense, what functions behind the central clash in *Vassilikos* is the arrogance of nobility, of a stern aristocracy that reminds one of Western Europe and of ancient Greece, however democratic the latter was. Venice, spreading its long shadow over the play, also liked to call itself a democracy. If one were to transfer the elements of the conflict to an ideological level, one would see the central clash in *Vassilikos* as that between prejudice and truth. This is in fact stated by Draghanighos, the opposite pole in the play. In the person of Ronkalas' son we recognize ideas of a somewhat later time, contemporary with the author, an influence of Rousseau rather than of Voltaire, which Matesis projects into his play as an acceptable anachronism. It is exactly this anachronism that makes the play, although set in the historical past, contemporary with its author. Rousseau's theory about personal property as the source of inequality among people is nowhere more evocatively depicted than in *Vassilikos*. Ronkalas' property consists, in his mind, not only of his belongings but of the members of his family.

"Wealth" and "blood," the elements of noble birth, are Darios' articles of faith; "justice" and "freedom" are those of Draghanighos. The latter's behavior is governed, as he tells us, by the mind and the heart. For Darios, vengeance is the cornerstone of one's honor. For him, as I have pointed out, honor and economic interest have an identical meaning. The foundation of the moral code of feudalism is purely economic, and here is where one can detect Matesis' progressive views.

Ronkalas is uneducated, and he ridicules his son for spending days and nights with books. The class that the *pater familias* in *Vassilikos* represents believes not in education, but in power. The conflict of views on honor and justice is nowhere expressed with more dramatic force than in the great scene of the last act which brings father and son face to face. It is a melancholy thought to remember the quality that these notions of justice and truth were one day to take in Robespierre's mouth. Fortunately for us, Matesis went behind the Thermidorean Terror which disfigured the French Revolution. He went straight to the humanistic origins of his values.

A humanist not only in words but in action as well, Draghanighos believes, as he says, that feudalism stood for barbarism. Both he and Gharoufalia possess a humanistic education, all the better assimilated for having been self-taught. We can imagine the brother reading to his sister in the evenings, as he mentions doing at one point. This has endowed Draghanighos with a precocious wisdom and a calm dignity. He is not an atheist. God for him is a purely spiritual principle. God is all wise and just, not a tyrant as Darios imagines him to be. The scene between Draghanighos and Gharoufalia in the second act, although the weakest in the play because too long and sententious, is the most enlightening from an ideological viewpoint. The monastic life that Darios wishes to impose upon Gharoufalia out of blind egotism and selfishness is indignantly opposed by Draghanighos, for no other reason than its being contrary to the wish, the inclinations, and the independence of his sister. Otherwise, Draghanighos considers monastic life as "indifferent to the philosopher," and by philosopher he means *moraliste*, which is the meaning that the word had in 18th-century France, the Age of Enlightenment.

Draghanighos is the ideal human type of the new age: serious, prudent, modest, thoughtful, with the kind of education that enables him to carry on his struggle against paternal arbitrariness with a degree of gentleness and respect. He represents the best promise that the progressive spirit can give us. If Darios Ronkalas is the aristocrat, Draghanighos is the true gentleman. How wonderful the world would be if it could convince us that the human type to come, after so much suffering and so many trials, was that represented by Draghanighos as drawn in 1830 by the gentle hand of Andonis Matesis, the poet of *Vassilikos*.

Thanasis Maskaleris

4. *Palamas and World Literature*

ONE of the most illuminating ways of approaching the work of Palamas is to examine it in relation to the heritage of western Europe, to single out the writers he admired most deeply and discover their influences on his work.[1] During his long and extremely active intellectual life, Palamas came into contact with a vast literary and philosophical tradition, and he assimilated a great variety of ideas. The protean quality of his work is the result of rich and diverse influences. From the time of his youth Palamas was an inspired student of classical literatures, and their effect on his development was profound. Similarly, he was influenced by oriental writings and the Bible. But the leading minds of the 19th century, particularly those of the last half, had the greatest impact on his personality. And it was through French literature and criticism that he was able to reach literatures otherwise inaccessible to him.

From the world outside Greece, Palamas needed ideas—"weapons," as he called them—in order to link Greece with Europe and the entire world and so achieve her modernization, backward as she was after her long slavery. This task of uniting Greece with the rest of the world through literature makes Palamas important from the point of view of world and comparative literature. Throughout his life Palamas followed Goethe's idea of *Weltliteratur*. He saw the literatures of the world as one whole, and he plunged into them with an acute awareness of their unbroken continuity and unity. He understood the fragmentation of man in the modern age and the need for universal ideas. His work was, among other

[1] This paper is a revised version of a chapter in *Kostis Palamas*, to be published in the Twayne World Authors Series.

things, an attempt to show the linking forces of humanity as they are manifested in literature. "The works of imagination in all times, and perhaps more in our age of immense development in communications, have been nurtured, in a sense, by mutual borrowings," he wrote in 1898, reflecting upon contemporary literary movements and influences.[2] His own poetic synthesis of the many diverse ideas that influenced him shows the unity and interdependence of a number of distinct literary streams. In his voluminous critical writings, literary traditions and writers are always presented in terms of their relations to each other, thus forming a continuous comparative study. In his criticism he constantly employs the method of comparison and contrast. "I love, I compare, I judge, I establish. These are the stages of criticism," he writes.[3] This statement sketches his entire critical function. With the word "love" he expresses not only the qualitative function of literary appreciation but also a quantitative embracing of works from all literatures. The word "compare" shows his passion for relating each literary work to the entire creation of the human mind. Then comes the evaluation, and finally the placement of the work in the body of world literature.

As Palamas' intellectual and spiritual world grew, he came to see himself and his work not only as part of the Greek tradition but also as part of the European and the world community. This vision enabled him to grasp the meaning of one humanity and one history, and led him to an idealistic panhumanism akin to Romain Rolland's. "The literary history of a people is a part of the immense

[2] Τὰ Πρῶτα Κριτικά (*First Critical Essays*), Athens, 1913, p. 193.
[3] Πεζοὶ Δρόμοι Α′ (*Paths in Prose*, vol. 1), Athens, 1928, p. 133.

literary body of the great European civilization, regardless of all its distinct temperamental and national characteristics," he writes,[4] and he means world civilization, where, in the context, he writes "European." Through a wide view of literature and all art, a world unity can be created. This is the essence of Palamas' universalism.

The Olympian personality of Goethe was for Palamas a source of constant inspiration. Before Solomos awakened him to the beauty of language and poetry, and before his European contemporaries inspired him with their dramatic conceptions of society and history, Goethe gave him the first stimulus toward poetic sublimation. For Palamas, Goethe's work was the perfect example of that classical unity which he struggled to attain all his life. The "great harmonizer," as he calls Goethe, taught him to seek the unity of the particular and the universal: "Our being is not yet filled with the wisdom of Goethe. There is no doubt that literature begins with the self, expresses the self, and is nothing without the self; but the most significant literary art is that which, without leaving the self isolated, is able to embrace, like the light, the entire external world."[5] This principle guides Palamas' poetry when he deals with both ideals and with actual social problems. And in the following lines about Goethe many of Palamas' own ideals are again reflected: "Among the towering figures of the century—mad, morbid, and convulsive because of their own greatness—stands the tranquil Olympian, strong and unshakable; he who came to know

[4] "Ποιητικὴ Τέχνη καὶ Γλώσσα" ("Poetic Art and Language"), Athens, 1908, p. 12. Ἅπαντα Η′ (*Works VIII*).

[5] Γράμματα Β′ (*The World of Letters*, vol. II), Athens, 1907, p. 17.

and shape in himself every ideal and all wisdom; who lived the life of all the past, resurrected the civilizations of all peoples and became the philosopher of all ideas and the singer of every emotion."[6]

This universality of Goethe—who is "everything in a high degree"—was the sun that illuminated Palamas' life and creative action. In his critical works and his introductions he constantly quotes Goethe, the teacher and guide of his thought. Goethe's maxim that those who have art and science have religion became an important principle in Palamas' life and a central theme in his work. And Goethe's cry, "Away from all that is dead; love what is living!" shaped one of Palamas' most fundamental attitudes toward his environment.

Palamas was also profoundly influenced by romantic poets whose temperaments and world views were radically different from those of Goethe. This is in agreement with his strong disapproval of the onesidedness of many contemporary poets who followed exclusively either the Byronic model or the classical side of Goethe. He observes that Goethe and Byron admired each other, and adds: "The greatness of the Goethean poet lies in his divine tranquility; the power of the Byronic springs from his satanic anger. The first has the weakness of coolness, the second that of sliding to the rhetorical."[7] In Palamas these two poetic temperaments are combined, and in his poetry we see a conscious attempt to avoid the extremes inherent in them. In Byron Palamas found the revolutionary spirit and the power of extreme individualism that he needed in his own struggles. The association of Byron with the

[6] *Ibid.*, p. 8.

[7] Πεζοὶ Δρόμοι Β′ (*Paths in Prose*, vol. II), Athens, 1928, p. 68.

Greek War of Independence and with Missolonghi, where Palamas lived as a child, kindled the love of the Greek poet for the English Romantic. "The poetry of Byron is great," he writes, "but Byron the man is, in a sense, greater than his poetry."[8] As with Palamas, so with Greece; the heroic life of Byron became a source of inspiration for freedom and action.

Victor Hugo was another poet who inspired Palamas with his romantic fire. Hugo, like Byron, was actively concerned with the fate of contemporary Greece, and this concern brought Palamas and other Greek writers even closer to him and to the romantic spirit in general. In an essay entitled "Victor Hugo and Greece," Palamas shows Hugo's relation to Greece and at the same time the relation of the romantic and the classical world views. The poet who did not seek perfection but the "immensity of things" achieved harmony in the sublimity of his expression and may be considered classical in the sense that he achieved an expression of the whole. "The secret of Hugo's art lies precisely in his total expression—the 'word of the Highest' as he calls it. So many others before and after him have known this 'word' incompletely; he expressed it entire."[9] In the love of Hugo for Greece—classical and eternal Greece—Palamas sees the classical side of romanticism and indicates the common ideals of classicism and romanticism: truth and beauty. Hugo's poetic-cultural movement from the Greece of Byron's grave to that of Sophocles ("Le Chant du Sophocle à Salamis") Palamas compares with the time movement from the present to the distant origins of romanticism.

[8] *Ibid.*, p. 88.

[9] *Ibid.*, p. 135.

"The sources of Romanticism," he writes, "are buried in the depths of the past."[10] This conception is part of Palamas' attempt to relate the classical and romantic views of life. Still writing about Hugo, Palamas defines poetry as: ". . . the logos that gives flesh to immaterial things and makes the worldly immaterial; the logos that gives form to the idea and measureless sublimity to form. . . . Of such a function of poetry the careful student of Hugo becomes profoundly aware."[11]

Hugo is for Palamas both the *patridolatre* and the cosmopolitan poet who said "un poète est un monde enfermé dans un homme," and "j'aime tous les soleils et toutes les patries." And Palamas himself both expressed and lived this ideal:

> I am a citizen of the world
> and the earth is my fatherland.
> *(Poems out of Season)*

and:

> I am a man; nothing that is human is strange to me
> and I may become familiar with everything.
> And since my fatherland is a world,
> the world too is a fatherland.
> (*Altars*—"The Airplane")

But above all Palamas saw Hugo as a giant fighting for the popular language and for democratic ideals. The moral support of this fighter, who suffered for his people and his ideas, was for Palamas, the demotic revolutionary, a powerful force of inspiration. Byron and Hugo influenced

[10] *Ibid.*, p. 98.

[11] *Ibid.*, p. 131.

Palamas more significantly in his early, revolutionary period. But the individualism of the first, and the universalism and humanism of the second, left permanent marks on his personality.

In the Parnassian poets Palamas found the kind of thought and poetry that satisfied the classical side of his temperament. From them, and particularly from Leconte de Lisle, he took the idea of a pure poetry that demands "la vénération de l'art, le dédain des succès faciles." Leconte de Lisle's constant preoccupation with the demands of form interested Palamas primarily. He too, like the strict Parnassian master, sought perfection of form and labored painstakingly to achieve it. "Perfect poetry," he writes, "exists only in verses of perfect workmanship."

The depth and breadth of Leconte de Lisle's thought was also of importance for Palamas, the "thoughtful singer." The epic imagination of Leconte de Lisle surveyed the historical past of humanity and recreated rhythmically the old forms of life and thought. Similarly, Palamas plunged into the history and lore of many peoples in order to draw material for his poetry; but, like Hugo, he gave a modern meaning to past situations and forms of life, while Leconte de Lisle remained entirely in the historical context of his visions. It was therefore Leconte de Lisle's formal and philosophical side that influenced Palamas; his extreme intellectual objectivity could not significantly affect the subjective side of the Greek poet. To Flaubert's doctrine of form and of the impersonality of art, Palamas reacted in a similar, negative manner.

Among the Parnassians, Sully Prudhomme is the poet closest to Palamas' poetic temperament. In him Palamas saw a reflection of himself, particularly in the late Prudhomme, who, like Anatole France, broke away from the Parnassians and concerned himself with the moral and philosophical problems of his time. The philosophical *aspiration* of Prudhomme, as contrasted to Leconte de Lisle's aim of *représentation*, is one of the chief strains in Palamas' work. He writes as follows about Prudhomme: "He thinks highly of the purpose of his art. The poet, he holds, must present in his verse the highest and the deepest questions of life. He is not, as they have called him, a 'singer of nature' but a singer of the human spirit. He does not only paint man's great sentiments, but above all he analyzes the minute quivers of the emotions."[12]

In these lines Palamas reveals both himself and his affinity with Prudhomme. But it is in the symbolism of the two poets that their similarity is most apparent. Their symbols are mainly ornamental images with a definite mythological or natural content but without the abstract autonomy, the musical suggestiveness, and the penetrating sharpness of the Baudelairian symbol. Palamas was also influenced by several other representatives of the diverse and constantly changing Parnassian group, particularly Gautier, Heredia, Baudelaire, Ménard, and Anatole France, but, again, the influence was limited to their characteristic insistence on formal perfection.

Along with the Parnassians, Palamas thoroughly studied the French symbolist poets, and he was the leading figure in introducing symbolism to Greece. He did not, however, respond to their theories as strongly as he did to those of the Parnassians. This is true of the response of Greek poets in general; symbolism never became truly native to Greece because of the lack of affinity between the

[12] Πεζοὶ Δρόμοι Α′ (*Paths in Prose*, vol. 1), p. 95.

Greek spiritual climate and the symbolist mood. The brilliance and transparency of the Greek landscape are qualities that do not favor the symbolist mood of closed space and exotic spiritual voyages. The world of Greece favors a plastic poetry rather than a musical one. The intense sunlight and the harmonious land and seascapes keep man a captive of the immediate and do not spur him to search for the exotic regions of the spirit. The symbols of Palamas are drawn from the concrete environment, and they are auxiliary forces in his poetry, never an end in themselves, as are the symbols of Baudelaire. Therefore the chief influence of symbolism on Palamas, and his contemporaries in general, was again one of creating greater respect for form and the spiritual significance of art. Another influence of the symbolists was effected through their exaltation of the word.

Palamas speaks with particular enthusiasm about Frédéric Mistral, whose poetry in the modern Provençal idiom he passionately admired. The two poets have many common characteristics of personality and poetics, and, in addition, filled similar positions with regard to their respective poetic traditions. Mistral's contribution to the enrichment of the Provençal tongue parallels Palamas' enrichment of the demotic. Both poets share a peculiar classic-romantic temperament, which is often found in the Graeco-Latin peoples of the Mediterranean coast (Camus the "pagan" is a striking, recent example of this temperament). Palamas translated Mistral's *Mirèio* and several other poems, and he considered him one of the leading poets of the age.

Anatole France is another writer whom Palamas studied with devotion. He was primarily inspired by the early pagan and classical works of France, such as *Les Noces corinthiennes* and *Thaïs*. The simultaneous interest of Palamas in the Christian and classical cultures was enkindled by France's similar pursuits. Palamas was particularly fascinated by France's ability to blend many diverse elements of thought and color.

Among Palamas' contemporary writers the Belgian poet Emile Verhaeren can best be compared with him. In their poetry one experiences the same uncontrollable passion that springs from their vision of modern man in a world dominated by science. Both were influenced by Renan's and Guyau's philosophical conceptions of science, and their enthusiasm for the modern age created a lyricism filled with images from the technological realm long before the arrival of the futurists. They are both pantheists, lovers of nature, and visionaries of future superior men. Their humanism and optimism spring from a vision of the future and from the admiration of human intelligence. Both poets developed free verse to a high order of beauty and were above all lyrical poets. But their most striking similarity is that, while intensely interested in the external world, they are dramatic poets of the interior—lyricists of the tormented self. As one critic of Verhaeren writes: "All the events and adventures of his life are of a psychological—an inner—order; all the defeats and victories are in his soul."[13] The same is true of Palamas. In this subjective mold both poets expressed the aspirations of our age and gave an epic grandeur to many elements of modern life. Amy Lowell has said that Verhaeren ". . . made poetry realize the modern world" and ". . . made us understand

[13] Enid Starkie, *Les Sources du lyrisme dans la poésie d'Emile Verhaeren*, Paris, 1927, p. 319.

that art and science are never at variance."[14] Palamas' contribution in this area is similar, perhaps even equal, to Verhaeren's.

Above all European writers of the last half of the 19th century, Palamas values Tolstoy, Ibsen, and Nietzsche. The significant differences in the world views of these "idol breakers," as he calls them, do not stop Palamas from considering them prophets of one world toward which humanity is evolving. In Tolstoy Palamas sees the moral rebel who brings a new "gospel" to mankind. What concerns him most in the work of Tolstoy is the problem of harmonizing individual and social morality. And, in Palamas' love for the Greek peasants and the demotic tradition, one sees elements of Tolstoy's "populism." Tolstoy's ideas about the human soul also had a strong influence on Palamas. "The writings of Tolstoy make us think every moment about the true value of life and above all about what is most significant according to the measure of the soul," he writes;[15] and he considers Tolstoy a poet of the natural and the moral man, who moves toward completeness through his moral growth.

Ibsen was for Palamas the greatest hero of social reform and the finest example of the modern social artist. The revolutionary ideas of Ibsen are found in many works of Palamas, particularly in his play *Trisevyene* and in *The Dodecalogue of the Gypsy*. The Gypsy and Ibsen's Brand grew out of a similar moral crisis—out of spiritual bondage and a sense of cultural decay—and both seek freedom and spiritual growth. The Gypsy is, like Brand, a torch endeavoring to fire the souls of his fellow tribesmen. The

[14] *Six French Poets*, New York, 1915, p. 47.

[15] Πεζοὶ Δρόμοι Α′ (*Paths in Prose*, vol. 1), p. 174.

Gypsy's search for self-knowledge is also reminiscent of Peer Gynt's search for his soul. Finally, one of the most striking qualities of Palamas is that which he himself attributed to Ibsen: ". . . a double-faced Janus, now social and now individualist."[16]

In Nietzsche's philosophy Palamas found many ideas which helped him to solve his psychological and artistic problems. Constantly living the antagonisms of the Apollonian and Dionysian forces, of classical Hellenism and Christianity, Palamas found in Nietzsche's writings ideas that inspired him to explore these antagonisms further. Like Nietzsche, he criticized his culture and worked for its regeneration. Nietzsche's ideas of asceticism and of the relationship of the individual to the mass are clearly echoed in *The Dodecalogue*; the Gypsy as a moral and cultural *agonistes* is a brother of Zarathustra. His love of the earth and the forests and his hatred of the cities are reminiscent of Zarathustra's words: "I love the forest. It is bad to live in the cities: there one finds too many of the lustful."[17] The feelings of the Gypsy as he breaks away from society are not without a Zarathustrian touch. A close comparison of the Gypsy and Zarathustra would reveal numerous affinities in mood and spirit.

Many other writers—especially D'Annunzio, Pascoli, Unamuno, Hardy, and William James—stimulated Palamas' thought and contributed to the creation of his protean art. The brief treatment of influences in this essay is by no means complete. The emphasis, as far as the influence of ideas is concerned, has been placed on non-Greek sources. Palamas' richest sources, however, are in the Greek tradi-

[16] *Ibid.*, p. 181.

[17] *The Philosophy of Nietzsche*, New York, 1927, p. 56.

tion. In ancient Greek and Byzantine writings and in the folk tradition he found an inexhaustible treasure of ideas, language, and metrical forms that he used and perfected. No other Greek writer, with the possible exception of Kazantzakis, can equal Palamas in his ability to draw creatively from the virgin regions of Greek language and life.

Edmund Keeley

5. *The "New" Poems of Cavafy*

IT is not surprising that the publication of seventy-five so-called new poems by C. P. Cavafy proved to be the major literary event of 1968 in Athens, indeed one of the truly significant events of the postwar period in Greek letters.[1] Since Cavafy is now fully recognized by his countrymen as the most original Greek poet of this century, any discovery concerning him is obviously important news. What does seem a bit surprising is the particular kind of excitement that the new poems initially inspired in Greece and that they have now begun to inspire in the United States, where Cavafy was virtually unknown before Lawrence Durrell brought the poet's ghost into the "Alexandria Quartet" late in the 1950's and W. H. Auden revealed, a few years later, that Cavafy had been an influence on his writing for over thirty years.[2] The initial response to the new poems among some critics in Greece had a touch of hysteria in it. Was it really proper for these poems to appear over the poet's dead body, so to speak? Would the new poems broaden or diminish his reputation? Could they in any case find a legitimate place in the

[1] The poems were published under the title *'Ανέκδοτα Ποιήματα, 1882-1923*, by the firm of Ikaros, under the editorship of George Savidis. I am indebted to Professor Savidis for his collaboration in both the translations that appear in this essay and those portions of the essay and the notes which are based on the introduction to *C. P. Cavafy: Passions and Ancient Days*, trans. Edmund Keeley and George Savidis, The Dial Press, New York, 1971. Much of my contribution to the critical remarks in this introduction originated in the commentary that I offered during a reading of the new poems at the Modern Greek Studies Association symposium held in Princeton.

[2] In his introduction to *The Complete Poems of Cavafy*, trans. Rae Dalven, New York, 1961.

Cavafy canon, so long established? Were some of the poems really as good as they seemed?

Perhaps the most effective answer to these doubts has come from younger readers approaching Cavafy's work for the first time during the several years since the newly discovered poems appeared in Athens. Professor George Savidis, Cavafy's Greek editor, reports that his students at the University of Salonika generally preferred the new poems to the old because some of the new poems seemed to speak with a clarity, honesty, and progressive spirit that are even more in keeping with a contemporary point of view than the most mature and advanced poems in the Cavafy canon, and this though the "new" poems in question were written for the most part near the turn of the century, that is, relatively early in Cavafy's poetic career.

It is also the young who are largely responsible for the astonishing progress of the poet's reputation in the United States, beginning with the generation of student readers brought up on Durrell and what came to be called the Alexandrian sensibility[3] and gaining sustenance from the interest of a number of younger American poets who discovered something of Cavafy's unique voice in the several translations that appeared early in the 1960's and who now recognize him as a major influence on their work.[4] The poet Mark Strand offers an example of this

[3] As first defined by Francis Golffing in "The Alexandrian Mind," *Partisan Review* (Winter 1955).

[4] The first translation of Cavafy to appear in the United States was John Mavrogordato's *The Poems of C. P. Cavafy*, New York, 1952. It was almost totally ignored by reviewers and soon became unavailable. The two translations that appeared in 1961, by Rae Dalven, *op.cit.*, and by Edmund Keeley and Philip Sherrard in

recognition in the preface to his 1969 anthology, *The Contemporary American Poets* (Meridian Books), when he speaks of a new generation of poets in the United States "whose imaginative roots seem to have sprung from Neruda or Char or Cavafy . . . quite as much as they have from Emerson or Whitman." And the 1970 Pulitzer Prize poet, Richard Howard, in commenting on the English-language edition of the new poems, writes of Cavafy's spreading influence in an even broader sense:

"He is the first Greek poet since Euripides we read with that kind of demonic self-recognition. He has influenced any poet who reads him, indeed it is correct to say he influences any reader, for Cavafy is among the few, the very few, writers who return us to the true meaning of 'influence': an astrological implication, the pressure of a fatality upon our lives. . . . Cavafy is one of the great writers we turn to . . . not because he delights us or because he demands our attention (though he does these things as well as they have ever been done), but because he comes to terms, answerable terms, with that relation to our own lives we most mistrust and evade—the relation to loss."[5]

Cavafy's persistent attempt to confront the truth, however painful, and to express it convincingly rather than settle for easy evasions, is what may best explain his popularity with the current younger generation. That he did not succeed to his own satisfaction is clear from one of the more personal of the new poems, "*Κρυμμένα*" ("Hidden Things," 1908). We sense here the long torment that

---

Six Poets of Modern Greece, were treated much more generously and served to introduce Cavafy to a wider audience.

[5] Quoted from the jacket of the first hardback edition of *C. P. Cavafy: Passions and Ancient Days.*

went into his effort to tell things the way they were, and we also find him carrying his search for the truth to an ultimate possibility as it applies to the poet himself: an honest admission that "all the things [he] said" finally masked the real truth, which was to be found only in his most veiled writing:

> *Ἀπ' ὅσα ἔκαμα κι ἀπ' ὅσα εἶπα*
> *νὰ μὴ ζητήσουνε νὰ βροῦν ποιὸς ἤμουν.*
> *Ἐμπόδιο στέκονταν καὶ μεταμόρφωνε*
> *τὲς πράξεις καὶ τὸν τρόπο τῆς ζωῆς μου.*
> *Ἐμπόδιο στέκονταν καὶ σταματοῦσε με*
> *πολλὲς φορὲς ποὺ πήγαινα νὰ πῶ.*
> *Οἱ πιὸ ἀπαρατήρητές μου πράξεις*
> *καὶ τὰ γραψίματά μου τὰ πιὸ σκεπασμένα—*
> *ἀπὸ ἐκεῖ μονάχα θὰ μὲ νοιώσουν.*
> *Ἀλλὰ ἴσως δὲν ἀξίζει νὰ καταβληθεῖ*
> *τόση φροντὶς καὶ τόσος κόπος νὰ μὲ μάθουν.*
> *Κατόπι—στὴν τελειοτέρα κοινωνία—*
> *κανένας ἄλλος καμωμένος σὰν ἐμένα*
> *βέβαια θὰ φανεῖ κ' ἐλεύθερα θὰ κάμει.*

> From all the things I did and all the things I said
> let no one try to find out who I was.
> An obstacle was there transforming
> the actions and the manner of my life.
> An obstacle was often there
> to silence me when I began to speak.
> From my most unnoticed actions
> and my most veiled writing—
> from these alone will I be understood.
> But maybe it isn't worth so much concern

and so much effort to discover who I really am.
Later, in a more perfect society,
someone else made just like me
is certain to appear and act freely.

The language of this poem (in the original) is as direct and unpretentious as any Cavafy used. It seems entirely consistent with both the poet's impulse to tell the full truth about himself and with the self-recognition implicit in his admission of failure.

Why did not his impulse in this direction move him to publish the poem during his lifetime, along with several others that are more specifically personal and more explicit than anything we find in the Cavafy canon? The poem itself suggests a partial answer: in his published work Cavafy normally chose to reveal his insight about himself and the human condition not through overt poetic statement, as in this poem, but through poetic veils and masks—that is, through characters and incidents set in a dramatic context, often historically distant yet at the same time often emblematic of contemporary attitudes. Another partial answer is that the distinction between published and unpublished work remained consistently blurred in Cavafy's case. In fact, he never actually published any of his poems in the sense of offering a volume of them commercially. As George Seferis has said, his poetry constituted a life-long "work in progress"[6] that reached the outside world largely through offprints or broadsheets distributed to friends and relatives. Although Cavafy began writing at the age of 19, his first printed pamphlet of

[6] See *On the Greek Style*, trans. Rex Warner and Th. Frangopoulos, Boston, 1966, p. 125.

poems did not appear until he was 41, and this "publication," issued in one hundred copies, consisted of only fourteen poems out of the several hundred he had written by that date: a kind of free sampler for those few who might care to try his poetry.[7] Throughout the rest of his life he promulgated his work largely by distributing folders that contained offprints or broadsheets held together by a huge clip, with a list of the contents in each kept up-to-date in his own hand. When the clips became overburdened, he would have some of the offprints withdrawn and sewn at his expense into booklets to accompany the ever-expanding folders. This process was repeated several times so that, at the poet's death in 1933, his "work in progress," still privately circulated, consisted of two sewn booklets containing a total of sixty-eight poems arranged thematically, and a folder of sixty-nine more recent poems arranged in order of first printing. At no point during his lifetime did Cavafy prepare a volume of his work for sale, and although his death was far from sudden, he left no definite instructions for the publication of a collected edition of his poems.

As this history suggests, Cavafy practiced an uncommon aesthetic asceticism throughout his life. And, to the end, he maintained a strong sense of the tentative about his work. Although he faithfully recorded the birth-date and title of each new-born poem in a private catalogue, he never considered a poem finished until he actually saw it in print, and even then it was subject to possible emenda-

[7] Cavafy really located the beginning of his creative maturity at the age of 48 by dividing his oeuvre into those poems written before 1911 and those he went on writing until 1932, the year before his death.

tion or rejection (an obvious advantage of the eccentric mode he chose for distributing his work). At the same time, a poem retained in manuscript form among his papers was always open to revision and ultimate publication, sometimes after undergoing a fifteen- or twenty-year period of trial; and among Cavafy's notes we find evidence that he returned regularly to his papers to dig out an early poem or an incomplete draft that might become the basis for publishable work.[8]

We can surmise, then, that most of the seventy-five "new" poems constituted that remnant of possibly redeemable work that Cavafy retained among his papers for ultimate revision and publication or as a source for new work. The fact is that any one of these unpublished poems could have gone the way of others that were destroyed. Their having been preserved would seem to indicate a definite continuing interest on Cavafy's part, as would the label "Not for publication but may remain here" (i.e., among the papers) that the poet attached to a number of them—and remain they did until some thirty years after his death, when his heir, Alexander Singopoulos, finally decided that the poet's reputation was secure enough to survive the publication of those distinctly inferior (not to say trivial) poems included in the volume of previously uncollected verse.[9]

[8] The poem "In Church," for example, was first written in 1892, revised in 1901, revised again in 1906, and finally published in 1912. "If Dead Indeed" had an even longer gestation: from a first version in 1897 to publication in 1920. The following marginal comment on one of Cavafy's unpublished poems illustrates his capacity for reconsidering early work left in limbo: "A very old poem: can anything be made of this?"

[9] Singopoulos did not include any of the 75 in the first collected edition of Cavafy's poems that he published in Alexandria in 1935

Since some of the new poems are clearly good enough in the form we find them to stand beside Cavafy's maturest work, the most plausible and least partial explanation for their having been designated "Not for publication" must remain the poet's feeling that they were simply too personal, or too explicit sexually, or too progressive for the taste of his particular community of readers, however much closer to an open expression of the truth they may have been than related poems in the canon. The new poem "Δυνάμωσις" ("Growing in Spirit," 1903), for ex-

---

(the edition that became the basis for the Cavafy canon) because he apparently felt that he ought to honor the poet's tacit wish to keep the unpublished poems out of print at least until they could in no way diminish the image of the poet that his heir hoped to promulgate in the years following his death. It must have been clear to Singopoulos that a number of the poems Cavafy retained among his papers were hardly more than early exercises of small artistic merit (though ultimately of possible interest to the literary biographer). Singopoulos, constantly protective of the poet's image, did not give anyone access to the papers in his possession until after the Second World War, and even then the access he allowed was strictly controlled, so that no more than 12 previously unpublished poems came to light between 1948 and 1963, when the first definitive edition of Cavafy's works was commissioned in connection with the centenary of his birth. At that time Singopoulos permitted the designated editor of Cavafy's poems, George Savidis, full access to the papers, and an additional 63 unpublished poems were thus brought to light, for ultimate publication in the scholarly edition of the new poems that appeared in Athens in 1968. The English-language edition of these poems is limited to those 21 out of the 63 that the translators felt could stand beside the poems Cavafy chose to print during his maturity (with the exception of a few that simply did not come over adequately into English and two—"Parthen" and "Coins"—that had to be excluded because their essential linguistic preoccupations were beyond translation).

ample, presents a point of view so modern, so far ahead of the times in which it was written, that it is not difficult to see why Cavafy may have feared that it would subject him to critical attack if it were distributed during his lifetime.

Ὅποιος τὸ πνεῦμα του ποθεῖ νὰ δυναμώσει,
νὰ βγῇ ἀπ' τὸ σέβας κι ἀπὸ τὴν ὑποταγή.
Ἀπὸ τοὺς νόμους μερικοὺς θὰ τοὺς φυλάξει,
ἀλλὰ τὸ περισσότερο θὰ παραβαίνει
καὶ νόμους κ' ἔθιμα, κι ἀπ' τὴν παραδεγμένη
καὶ τὴν ἀνεπαρκοῦσα εὐθύτητα θὰ βγεῖ.
Ἀπὸ τὲς ἡδονὲς πολλὰ θὰ διδαχθεῖ.
Τὴν καταστρεπτικὴ δὲν θὰ φοβᾶται πρᾶξι·
τὸ σπίτι τὸ μισὸ πρέπει νὰ γκρεμισθεῖ.
Ἔτσι θ'ἀναπτυχθεῖ ἐνάρετα στὴν γνῶσι.

He who hopes to grow in spirit
will have to free himself from obedience and respect.
He'll hold to some laws
but he'll mostly violate
both law and custom, and go beyond
the established, inadequate norm.
Sexual pleasure will have much to teach him.
He won't be afraid of the destructive act:
half the house will have to come down.
This way he'll grow virtuously into wisdom.[10]

For a poet to declare that the road to virtue lies in living beyond the established norm, or to suggest that there is

[10] This translation and those that follow have been revised by me in collaboration with Philip Sherrard for inclusion in *C. P. Cavafy: Selected Poems*, Princeton University Press, 1972.

room for the destructive act, could be a hazardous position to take in the Greek world today, let alone in Alexandria at the turn of the century (though it is an attitude with obvious appeal to the younger generation in both Greece and the United States). At the same time, it would be a mistake to see Cavafy as a prophet of the extreme New Left, since he tells us that some laws must be honored and that only half the house must be pulled down. It is the poet's overt—not to say didactic—insistence on the virtue of pleasure that is the most substantial avant-garde element in the poem and that also relates it to a number of the best-known poems in the canon, this being perhaps the earliest expression of the "Ithaca" theme made famous by the later poem of that name.

Cavafy's erotic poems are also uniquely avant-garde for work written so early in this century. In his quest to tell the truth about life as he really experienced it, he became the first poet since Whitman to make homosexual love a central subject of his exploration, and his open treatment of the subject, sometimes so particular as to seem self-indulgent, makes Whitman's more ambiguous treatment appear a kind of evasion. Cavafy's eroticism becomes most illuminating when the focus of his concern is not so much an honest depiction of particular encounters or affairs as it is an honest dramatization of those vital and complex tensions that are manifest to some degree in all erotic experience. The best of the new erotic poems concentrate on the inescapable tension between illusion and reality, or imagination and actuality, in the game of love. At moments illusion is seen as a palliative for the loss of a reality that was almost achieved but that remained unrealized: a reality that is seen to be very much worth achieving. At other moments, the reality of love seems to reside not so much in palpable experience as in images that the mind is stimulated to construct by an erotic impulse.

In "At the Theatre," for example, the theatrical performance that most enraptures the speaker is that of his own imagination in "picturing" the object of his attention "the way they'd talked about [him] that afternoon." Again, in "The Photograph," the speaker dismisses the crude (and probably heterosexual) reality of an obscene photograph in order to preserve, for the purposes of his art, a dreamlike image of the figure shown there, a figure "shaped for and dedicated to Hellenic love." We find a more extreme variation on the same theme in "On Hearing of Love," where the speaker actually designates real and tangible loves as lesser to those which the imagination creates. But the most persuasive dramatization of the theme is that of "Μισὴ Ὥρα" ("Half an Hour," 1917), one of the most memorable erotic poems that Cavafy wrote in any year:

> *Μήτε σὲ ἀπέκτησα, μήτε θὰ σὲ ἀποκτήσω*
> *ποτέ, θαρρῶ. Μερικὰ λόγια, ἕνα πλησίασμα*
> *ὅπως στὸ μπὰρ προχθές, καὶ τίποτε ἄλλο.*
> *Εἶναι, δὲν λέγω, λύπη. Ἀλλὰ ἐμεῖς τῆς Τέχνης,*
> *κάποτε μ' ἔντασι τοῦ νοῦ, καὶ βέβαια μόνο*
> *γιὰ λίγην ὥρα, δημιουργοῦμεν ἡδονὴν*
> *ἡ ὁποία σχεδὸν σὰν ὑλικὴ φαντάζει.*
> *Ἔτσι στὸ μπὰρ προχθὲς—βοηθῶντας κιόλας*
> *πολὺ ὁ εὐσπλαχνικὸς ἀλκολισμὸς—*
> *εἶχα μισὴ ὥρα τέλεια ἐρωτική.*
> *Καὶ τὸ κατάλαβες μὲ φαίνεται,*
> *κ' ἔμεινες κάτι περισσότερον ἐπίτηδες.*

Ἦταν πολλὴ ἀνάγκη αὐτό. Γιατὶ
μ' ὅλην τὴν φαντασία, καὶ μὲ τὸ μάγο οἰνόπνευμα,
χρειάζονταν νὰ βλέπω καὶ τὰ χείλη σου,
χρειάζονταν νά'ναι τὸ σῶμα σου κοντά.

I never had you nor, I suppose,
will I ever have you. A few words, an approach,
as in the bar yesterday—nothing more.
It's sad, I admit. But we who serve Art,
sometimes with the mind's intensity
can create pleasure that's almost physical—
but of course only for a short time.
That's how in the bar yesterday—
mercifully helped by alcohol—
I had half an hour that was totally erotic.
And I think you understood this
and stayed slightly longer on purpose.
It was necessary, that. Because
with all the imagination, all the magic alcohol,
I needed to see your lips as well,
I needed your body near me.

The poem opens with what seems a thoroughly sincere expression of regret on the speaker's part over his having failed to realize a tangible reality in the situation described. Yet very soon the regret is qualified crucially by complex implications: sometimes, by intensity of mind, the artist can create an imagined pleasure that, though short-lived, is *almost* physical, and this less than physical experience of the imagination is nevertheless total, even perfect (the Greek permits either rendering). One is led to wonder whether the speaker, for all his stated sadness, would make the same claim for any actual, realized experience he may have had. What he implies is that the artist, through the intensity of his imagination, can know that which the lover will probably never know, however tangible and however realized the lover's passion. At the same time, he suggests that the imagination must always be rooted in a physical reality. The poem concludes with the implication that however total or perfect the imagined experience may have been in this instance, it still required an almost tangible consciousness of the loved one's physical presence to be as real as it was.

In an anonymous commentary on his work, Cavafy once identified the three principal modes of his poetry as the erotic, the philosophical, and the historical.[11] The first two are frequently interwoven, as in the above poem, and occasionally all three come together in a single work; but the historical mode was Cavafy's favorite, and it dominates both the new and the previously collected verse. The poet himself is reported to have said, toward the end of his life, that he felt he could never write a novel or a play, but that he heard inside him a hundred and twenty-five voices telling him that he could write history.[12]

What Cavafy chose to write in fact can be described as a collection of historical epiphanies in verse: the evocation of moments that suddenly illuminate the essential truth about a known historical figure or a celebrated historical event, or the evocation of imaginary figures and imaginary occasions, often outside the mainstream of history but sig-

[11] See G. P. Savidis, Οἱ Ἐκδόσεις τοῦ Καβάφη (*The Editions of Cavafy*), Athens, 1966, p. 209.

[12] M. Peridis, Ὁ Βίος καὶ τὸ Ἔργο τοῦ Κωνσταντίνου Καβάφη (*The Life and Work of Cavafy*), Athens, 1948, p. 121.

nificant for the commentary they offer on analogous occasions in the present. In the latter case, history became the source of Cavafy's myth, his means for "manipulating a continuous parallel between contemporaneity and antiquity," to use Eliot's famous comment on Joyce's *Ulysses*. We find an example of the former case, a more or less "pure" historical epiphany, in the new poem called "Τὸ τέλος τοῦ Ἀντωνίου" ("Antony's Ending," 1907), which immediately calls to mind several of the more familiar historical poems in the canon having to do with Alexandria during Cleopatra's reign. Here, instead of diminishing Antony from the ironic perspective of those watching him parade superfluities, as in "Alexandrian Kings," or admonishing him to rise up with courage so as to be worthy of the Greek city he has known so well, as in "The God Abandons Antony," Cavafy portrays this defeated Roman almost as though he were a morally triumphant Greek—a Demetrios Soter or a Manuel Komnenos or the Spartan mother of King Kleomenes—ready to confront his fall from grace with the knowledge of who he really is and with full pride in this knowledge:

> Ἀλλὰ σὰν ἄκουσε ποὺ ἐκλαῖγαν οἱ γυναῖκες
> καὶ γιὰ τὸ χάλι του ποὺ τὸν θρηνοῦσαν,
> μὲ ἀνατολίτικες χειρονομίες ἡ κερά,
> κ' οἱ δοῦλες μὲ τὰ ἑλληνικὰ τὰ βαρβαρίζοντα,
> ἡ ὑπερηφάνεια μὲς στὴν ψυχή του
> σηκώθηκεν, ἀηδίασε τὸ ἰταλικό του αἷμα,
> καὶ τὸν ἐφάνηκαν ξένα κι ἀδιάφορα
> αὐτὰ ποὺ ὥς τότε λάτρευε τυφλὰ—
> ὅλ' ἡ παράφορη Ἀλεξανδρινὴ ζωή του—
> κ' εἶπε "Νὰ μὴν τὸν κλαῖνε. Δὲν ταιριάζουν τέτοια.

Μὰ νὰ τὸν ἐξυμνοῦνε πρέπει μᾶλλον,
πού ἐστάθηκε μεγάλος ἐξουσιαστής,
κι ἀπέκτησε τόσ' ἀγαθὰ καὶ τόσα.
Καὶ τώρα ἂν ἔπεσε, δὲν πέφτει ταπεινά,
ἀλλὰ Ρωμαῖος ἀπὸ Ρωμαῖο νικημένος".

But when he heard the women wailing,
lamenting his sorry state—
madam with her oriental gestures
and her slaves with their barbarous Greek—
the pride in his soul rose up,
his Italian blood sickened with disgust
and all he'd worshipped blindly till then—
his wild Alexandrian life—
now seemed dull and alien.
And he said: "Stop wailing for me.
It's all wrong, that kind of thing.
You ought to be singing my praises
for having been a great ruler,
a man of wealth and glory.
And if I'm down now, I haven't fallen humbly,
but as a Roman conquered by a Roman".

One senses something of Cavafy's lifelong familiarity with alienation in this poem. As a Greek born in Alexandria, educated largely in England and Constantinople, and destined to spend the best part of his life as a member of the Greek community in Egypt rather than in mainland Greece, he remained obsessed with defining both that which was essentially Greek in him and that which was a product of his separation from the center of the Greek world. George Seferis tells us that Cavafy insisted on proclaiming: "I am not a Greek. I am a Hellene"; but exactly what it means to be a Hellene became a major preoccupation of his verse.[13] At one extreme we find poems that seem to propose an almost mystical conviction that to be Hellenic is the closest one can come to being godly on this earth, and to lose that quality is a kind of fall from earthly paradise:

> . . . he was that superlative thing: Hellenic
> mankind has no finer quality;
> everything beyond that belongs to the gods.
>
> (From "Epitaph of Antiochos, King of Kommagini")

or:

> . . . but how they'd fallen, what they'd now become,
> living and speaking like barbarians,
> excluded—what a catastrophe—from the Hellenic way of life.
>
> (From "Poseidonians")[14]

At the other extreme we have the new poem "Returning from Greece" (1914), where the alienated Greek speaker

[13] George Seferis, *On the Greek Style*, p. 130. E. M. Forster was the first to identify some of the complexities of this preoccupation, in *Two Cheers for Democracy*, London, 1951, pp. 249-50: "[Cavafy] was a loyal Greek, but Greece for him was not territorial. It was rather the influence that has flowed from his race this way and that through the ages, and that (since Alexander the Great) has never disdained to mix with barbarism, has indeed desired to mix; the influence that made Byzantium a secular achievement. Racial purity bored him, so did political idealism. . . . The civilization he respected was a bastardy in which the Greek strain prevailed, and into which, age after age, outsiders would push, to modify and be modified."

[14] The full text of this new poem appears in *Passions and Ancient Days*.

admits, on returning from a visit to the mainland, that he is just as happy to be sailing through his home waters of Cyprus and Syria and Egypt because there he can give free play to the affections and emotions of Asia that are repugnant to Hellenism—in fact, perfect Hellenic honesty calls for him not only to honor but to glory in the unHellenic blood of Syria and Egypt "in [his] veins."

This ambiguity about exactly what it means to be truly Hellenic—about the affectation and snobbery that anything other than an ambiguous attitude apparently engenders—serves to color one of the very best of the new poems, "Φυγάδες" ("Exiles," 1914), where a contemporary analogue of the historical occasion comes in so pat as to make the poet appear to have been uncannily prophetic (the poem was written over fifty years before the military coup of 1967 created the current generation of political exiles in Paris). Here we are shown a group of Greeks from the mainland who have been dispossessed for political reasons and condemned for the time being to live in the "wonderful" city of Alexandria, where they attempt to create a plausible Greek world through excursions, a bit of study, and some talk of religion and literature, almost as they might at home. But what really keeps them alive during this "not unpleasant" stay abroad is their hope of an imminent return to the mother country, a hope that depends on friends moving to overthrow the Emperor Basil I (A.D. 867-886), who, history tells us, succeeded in never being overthrown at all:

Πάντα ἡ ᾿Αλεξάνδρεια εἶναι. Λίγο νὰ βαδίσεις
στὴν ἴσια της ὁδὸ ποὺ στὸ ῾Ιπποδρόμιο παύει,
θὰ δεῖς παλάτια καὶ μνημεῖα ποὺ θ᾿ ἀπορήσεις.

Ὅσο κι ἂν ἔπαθεν ἀπ' τοὺς πολέμους βλάβη
ὅσο κι ἂν μίκραινε, πάντα θαυμάσια χώρα.
Κ' ἔπειτα μ' ἐκδρομές, καὶ μὲ βιβλία,
καὶ μὲ σπουδὲς διάφορες περνᾶ ἡ ὥρα.
Τὸ βράδυ μαζευόμεθα στὴν παραλία
ἡμεῖς οἱ πέντε (μὲ ὀνόματα ὅλοι
πλαστὰ βεβαίως) κι ἄλλοι μερικοὶ Γραικοὶ
ἀπ' τοὺς ὀλίγους ὅπου μείνανε στὴν πόλι.
Πότε μιλοῦμε γιὰ ἐκκλησιαστικὰ (κάπως λατινικοὶ
μοιάζουν ἐδῶ), πότε φιλολογία.
Προχθὲς τοῦ Νόννου στίχους ἐδιαβάζαμε.
Τί εἰκόνες, τί ρυθμός, τί γλῶσσα, τί ἁρμονία.
Ἐνθουσιασμένοι τὸν Πανοπολίτην ἐθαυμάζαμε.
Ἔτσι περνοῦν οἱ μέρες, κ' ἡ διαμονὴ
δυσάρεστη δὲν εἶναι, γιατὶ, ἐννοεῖται,
δὲν πρόκειται νά'ναι παντοτεινή.
Καλὲς εἰδήσεις λάβαμε, καὶ εἴτε
ἀπὸ τὴν Σμύρνη κάτι γίνει τώρα, εἴτε τὸν Ἀπρίλιο
οἱ φίλοι μας κινήσουν ἀπ' τὴν Ἤπειρο, τὰ σχέδιά μας
ἐπιτυγχάνουν, καὶ τὸν ρίχνουμεν εὐκόλως τὸν Βασίλειο.
Καὶ τότε πιὰ κ' ἐμᾶς θά'ρθ' ἡ σειρά μας.

It goes on being Alexandria still. Just walk a bit
along its straight road ending at the Hippodrome
and you'll see palaces and monuments that will amaze you.
Whatever war-damage it's suffered,
however much smaller it's grown,
it's still a wonderful city.
And then, what with excursions and books
and various kinds of study, times does go by.
In the evenings we meet on the sea-front,
the five of us (all, naturally, under fictitious names)

and some of the few other Greeks
still left in the city.
Sometimes we discuss church affairs
(the people here seem to lean toward Rome)
and sometimes literature.
The other day we read some lines by Nonnos:
what imagery, what rhythm, what diction and harmony!
In our enthusiasm, how we admired the Panopolitan.
So the days go by, and our stay here
isn't unpleasant, because naturally
it's not going to last forever.
We've had good news: whether
something is happening now in Smyrna, or whether
in April our friends decide to move from Epiros,
our plans are definitely working out, and we'll easily
    overthrow Basil.
And when we do, at last our turn will come.[15]

The tone of the poem is characteristic: a speaker not entirely aware of what the poet and the reader know and thus vulnerable to a kind of dramatic irony. One suspects that it is his rather condescending attitude toward Alexandria that earned him this vulnerability. Aloof as the speaker may hope to remain during his sojourn in the provinces, confident as he may be of his turn back home on the mainland, the truth is that his fate has already condemned him to the provinces forever, and Cavafy slyly

[15] The scene is probably set shortly after the murder of Emperor Michael III by Basil I, his co-emperor at the time. The mention of Christians who "lean toward Rome" further points to the period of the Photian schism (867-870), when its initiator, the Patriarch of Constantinople, Photius, had been deposed by the Emperor and most of his friends had been driven into exile.

counts on our knowledge of this to keep the speaker in his place during our reading of the poem. In the end it is Alexandria that triumphs, as it so often does in Cavafy; the city will go on being Alexandria still some centuries after your fated exiles and their usurping emperors have become merely names for a footnote to a dramatic monologue.

These, then, are some of the best of Cavafy's "new" poems: alienated to a degree, unusually candid and progressive, cunningly ironic, sometimes as wise in their way as the mature poems he chose to print during his lifetime—in fact, sometimes less masked and more forthright than the most personal of his collected poems. Cavafy might turn over in his grave were he to learn that works he had assiduously kept out of print while he was alive may now serve to broaden the audience for his poetry as effectively as the increasingly popular poems that make up his collected edition. This seems to be happening in Greece; whether or not it can happen in the United States, where the poems are accessible to most only in translation, remains to be seen. But for this admittedly partial reader, there is no doubt that all twenty-one new poems offered in the English-language edition deserve a place among Cavafy's collected poems and that several extend our view of this remarkable poet in startling ways.

Peter Bien

6. *The Demoticism of Kazantzakis*

IN choosing the subject "The Demoticism of Kazantzakis," I hope to present Kazantzakis in a much broader way than that in which he is usually seen.[1] Most people in the English-speaking world know him only from his novels, which represent just the last sixteen years of his fifty-one-year career. And we know the novels only in translation. Even Greeks and others who read these books in the original may be unaware of Kazantzakis' earlier career and in particular of the role that the "language question" played in that career. My object therefore is really twofold: (a) to give a sense of Kazantzakis' zealous involvement with demotic, and (b) to give this sense over the entire length of his active professional life, from 1906 to 1957.

If we read Kazantzakis without this double perspective we do him a disservice and we also limit our understanding of Greek literary life in general, for the literary development of the past one hundred years has been intimately connected with linguistic controversy. In the case of Kazantzakis specifically, it is vital for us to realize that the problem of language obsessed him from the very start and that this obsession was one of the few constants stretching unchanged throughout all the other permutations of his career.

This vital concern must be stressed all the more because Kazantzakis himself was somewhat deceptive in this regard. Strangely, he says next to nothing about the language question in *Report to Greco*, his "spiritual autobiography." Also, he maintained a pose in which he

[1] The material in this essay is presented in greatly expanded form in the author's book "Kazantzakis and the Linguistic Revolution in Greek Literature," Princeton University Press, 1972.

denigrated all purely linguistic, literary, or aesthetic involvement; this is the pose in which he castigated himself as a "pen-pusher." But there is a great deal of evidence in out-of-the-way places to show his linguistic and aesthetic concern. Kazantzakis, who had equally strong needs for posing and for sincerity, continually gave himself away. Near the end of his career, for example, when he was in exile and found himself persecuted as a communist, traitor, and anti-Christ, he was provoked into hitting back, proudly shouting: "I am reviled as an EAM-Bulgarian and an unethical traitor. Immortal Greeks: I have sacrificed my entire life for the spirit of Greece; I have labored passionately in the Greek language and the Greek tradition. My conscience is clear. . . ."[2] In such a moment of extreme provocation, when truth will out, Kazantzakis spoke not of God or philosophy or even of politics, but of the linguistic drive within him: his involvement in demotic.

What I would like to do in this essay is to document this long involvement, to show its permutations and how it both hindered and fostered Kazantzakis' development as an artist. In the process of doing this I wish at the same time to put forth a thesis, as follows:

1. In the years roughly 1910-1920, Kazantzakis' demoticism existed in a suitable context, but his crusade took more of a political and pedagogical character than a literary one. This period ended in 1920 because it was then that Kazantzakis became severely disillusioned with Greece and began to see himself as a European, cosmopolitan writer.

2. In the years roughly 1920-1940, Kazantzakis con-

[2] Δῆμος Ἡρακλείου Κρήτης, Ἀναμνηστικὸ λεύκωμα Νίκου Καζαντζάκη, 1961, p. 31.

tinued his demoticism—indeed, language was often his sole link with a Greece that he otherwise disdained. This disdain was augmented because various of his projects on behalf of demotic were frustrated entirely or partially and because the texts that he did manage to publish in an "uncorrected" language were subjected to abuse. All this made him more intransigent than ever, and determined him to apply his exacerbated linguistic zeal to the *Odyssey*, turning it into a paradigm for spelling reform and a repository for thousands of words that might otherwise have been lost. But in its subject matter and ideology the *Odyssey* is very far from what might be called the demotic spirit; indeed some would say that the poem has nothing to do with Greek reality, except in its externals. In other words, Kazantzakis' demoticism—though now manifesting itself in literature and not in pedagogical reform or in politics—had not yet found a proper literary context.

3. In the years 1940-1957, years in which Kazantzakis renewed his love of Greece, he finally provided a better literary context for his crusading demoticism. This was in the late novels, which attempt to deal with everyday Greek life in a language congruent with the new subject-matter he had found.

When Kazantzakis arrived in Athens in 1906 to begin his career as a writer, he found himself in the midst of a linguistic and cultural revolution that had already gathered momentum. Ideally, I should now try to give some background to the language question: why the struggle for demotic arose, and in what stage it found itself when Kazantzakis came upon the scene. But this would require an extended study far transcending the scope of this essay.

Suffice it to say that by 1906 the movement had made great progress, especially in poetry, although demotic was by no means yet fully accepted in the theatre, and it had made no inroads whatsoever in scholarly writing or in the schools. Suffice it to say, also, that the movement had by this time thrown up distinct leaders such as Psycharis, whose book Τὸ Ταξίδι μου (*My Journey*) had launched the demotic revolution in 1888; the poet Palamas, then at the height of his prestige; and Ion Dragoumis, who became Kazantzakis' friend and one of the chief influences on him. The movement had also developed its organ of propaganda and persuasion in the crusading periodical *Noumas.*

When Kazantzakis arrived in Athens he was not an *extreme* demoticist. This position he developed in his first few years there, in response to the people and spirit he encountered. But it did not take him long to become a vocal participant in the movement; the first of his many demotic manifestoes was published in 1907.[3] Arguing the problem of whether so-called foreign words ought to be expelled from Greek, he asked quite sensibly: How can we know which words are "foreign" and which are not? Then he replied in what he called the only rational way: "Greek" words are those which live on the lips of the Greek people. Obviously, by this definition a living word of French derivation, such as *γάντι* (glove) or one borrowed long ago from Latin, such as *σπίτι* (house; from *hospitium*), is Greek, while impeccably Greek words that have fallen out of use are "foreign." He then exhorted the Greek people to break the chains of tradition, accept the contemporary spoken idiom, and stop being so chauvin-

[3] "Τὸ γλωσσικόν μας ζήτημα," Ἀκρόπολις, May 31, 1907, p. 2.

istic as far as language was concerned. English, French, and Spanish are full of loan words, he said. Why not Greek?

By 1909 he had identified himself with the extreme, radical demoticists, the so-called *malliari*. He informed his publisher that the *malliari* idiom was the only one in which he could "express vibrantly" what was circulating in his blood.[4] In the same year he became president of the Solomos Society of Irakleion, a group formed to work for the inclusion of demotic in the schools. The Society's manifesto, written by Kazantzakis, was published in June 1909 in *Noumas*.[5] It begins by stating the purpose of the Solomos Society: to convince Greeks that their written language should be based on the language they speak. As soon as a child enters school, Kazantzakis said, he is taught to scorn his maternal tongue. He must never write *ψωμὶ, νερὸ, κρασὶ, σπίτι*, but rather *ἄρτος, ὕδωρ, οἶνος, οἰκία*. The problem is that the teachers, blinded by the splendor of the ancient tongue, have forgotten that languages develop. Although it did not take long to discover the impossibility of returning to the idiom of Plato or even of Xenophon, teachers failed to take the reasonable step of abandoning *katharevousa* altogether; instead, they began making compromises, mixing the old and the new, with the result that thousands of different *katharevousas* exist. The worst aspect of the problem is that the words to be suppressed are the most living and common: terms for

[4] Πέτρου Μαρκάκη, "'Ανέκδοτα γράμματα τοῦ Νίκου Καζαντζάκη: Τὸ Περιοδικὸ Πινακοθήκη κι ὁ Δημ. Καλογερόπουλος," Καινούρια 'Εποχή (Autumn 1959), p. 38.

[5] Σύλλογος Δημοτικιστῶν 'Ηρακλείου Κρήτης "'Ο Σολωμός," 'Ο Νουμᾶς, June 7, 1909, pp. 9-12.

clothing—*καπέλλα, παντούφλες, γάντια, κάλτσες*; for the tools of the various trades; for the most familiar things in ourselves and our environment: *φωτιά* (*πῦρ*), *πόδι* (*πούς*), *χῶμα* (*χοῦς*), *χέρι* (*χείρ*), *αὐτὶ* (*οὖς*).

The consequences, continued Kazantzakis, are catastrophic. In the educational realm the child is made to feel confused, forced to learn words he will never hear. Socially, the consequences are equally bad. Instead of learning something of practical value in school, we learn ancient Greek—that is, we learn to hate it, because Homer, Plato, and the rest are forever connected in our minds with the terrors of syntax, parsing, declensions. With this as a start, we come to hate all books, all learning, and develop a society that despises all books and learning—a society without idealism. As far as the nation is concerned, bilingualism creates a split between the learned and the people, because the books the professors write can never be read by the ordinary man. Bilingualism thus destroys national unity and inhibits Greek progress.

In summary: "*Katharevousa* is unable to mold the child's spirit; it suffocates the mind and distorts the child's natural development. It makes us into superficial people full of hollow words and braggart phraseology; prevents us from loving books, study, everything serious and researched; breaks the nation's linguistic unity and little by little our very national integrity." Demoticists, Kazantzakis added, do not want to touch religion or coin new words; they merely want demotic to be the common, accepted language throughout Greece. This is possible because the differences existing in the various regions are lexical, not syntactical or grammatical. Demotic is a universal language for Greece, and it will triumph, just as a common idiom triumphed in Dante's Italy, Luther's Germany, and Lomonosov's Russia. Our opponents say: "Nothing is more perfect than the achievements of the ancient Greeks." We reply: "Life moves forward; it never turns back." Such was the manifesto Kazantzakis wrote for the Solomos Society in 1909.

We have seen that at the beginning of the period 1910-1920 Kazantzakis was active as a polemicist for the demotic cause. He was also writing: there is a novel done at this time (*Broken Souls*) and a play that won an important literary prize (*The Masterbuilder*), both in "pure" demotic; there is also a group of plays (*Odysseas, Nikiforos Phokas, Christos*) in all likelihood written in or around 1915, when Venizelos was out of office and Kazantzakis found his political activities restricted. But in general the decade 1910-1920 was essentially a non-literary one for Kazantzakis. His energies seemed to go everywhere at once. He busied himself with politics, educational reform, humanitarian service (the mission to the Caucasus), and even business (several ventures, including a singularly unremunerative attempt at mining with a foreman named George Zorbas).

As far as Kazantzakis' demoticism is concerned, however, the one area that we must consider is educational reform. The reformers wished to press their proposals in the most effective way possible, especially since the demoticist Venizelos was now in power. Thus, in 1910, they formed the Educational Association, a pressure group with the purpose of reforming Greek education linguistically, and building up a collection of texts, stories, histories, and workbooks so that, once the requisite laws had been passed, the teachers would have materials with which to work. Kazantzakis was the secretary of this association, and one of its founders. Although the demoticist proposals were defeated in Parliament during Venizelos' first period (1910-1915), the reformers had cause for optimism, since certain elements of their program were adopted by the Ministry of Education, and since the very fact of a debate in Parliament had constituted the first official recognition, as far as education was concerned, of the independent existence of modern Greek culture. As events turned out, the broad and public discussion had sown a seed which germinated soon afterward.[6]

In this favorable climate Kazantzakis began shifting his energies toward the writing of school primers in demotic. Specifically, in 1914 the Ministry of Education announced a competition for textbooks, and we find Kazantzakis collaborating with his wife Galatia on readers for the elementary grades. In 1915 five of these, all bearing Galatia's name as author, won prizes and were accordingly sanctioned by the Ministry.[7]

During the remainder of the decade his energies shifted first to business, as I have indicated, and then in 1919 to his service in the Venizelos government as Director-General in the Ministry of Welfare, with responsibility for repatriating 150,000 Caucasian Greeks who were being harassed by the Bolsheviks. Although he was not actively campaigning for demotic during this time, he was of course continuing to write in the *malliari* idiom and, more important, he was continuing the nationalism that went

[6] Α. Π. Δελμούζου, "Ὁ *δημοτικισμὸς καὶ ἡ ἐπίδρασή του στὴν Ἑλληνικὴ παιδεία*," *Νέα Ἑστία*, November 1, 1939, p. 1466.

[7] Ἔλλης Ἀλεξίου, *Γιὰ νὰ γίνει μεγάλος*, Athens, 1966, pp. 63 and 88.

hand-in-glove with his demoticism throughout this decade.

In 1920 came a decisive change. I cited Ion Dragoumis earlier as a key figure in the demotic movement and as one of the chief influences on Kazantzakis. In particular, it was Dragoumis who provided the model for Kazantzakis' nationalism. On August 13, 1920 (new style), the day the news of the assassination attempt on Venizelos in Paris reached Greece, Dragoumis was murdered on the streets by security police. This event shocked Kazantzakis deeply and confirmed him in an already growing disillusionment with Greek political life, a disillusionment that was completed two years later by the debacle in Asia Minor. In 1920, furthermore, Kazantzakis' position became impossible owing to Venizelos' defeat at the polls on November 14. Kazantzakis resigned his position in the Ministry, and a week later was on a train headed for Paris, inaugurating an entirely new phase in his career.

He now turned against his former nationalism, and displayed bitterness and scorn toward Greece and Greek aspirations. Henceforth, for almost fifteen years, he was to try to establish himself as a European writer. Politically, he was to convert his nationalism into communist internationalism. But the fall of Venizelos and the murder of Dragoumis did not shake his zeal for demotic. Although this had developed step by step along with his nationalism, it had by now become sufficiently autonomous to continue on its own, and it did indeed continue unabated. Actually, demoticism was the only aspect of Kazantzakis' belief or practice that never caused him doubts. The problem now was not his zeal, but how and where to apply it. In exile he was isolated from the fellowship of the other demoticists and removed from the natural context for his linguistic crusade. As so often happens in such cases, the result was the augmentation of his pugnaciousness, intransigence, and linguistic fanaticism. I stress this intransigence because I believe it to be a remote but determining factor in that fanaticism's most crucial manifestation: the language of the *Odyssey*. In reviewing Kazantzakis' efforts to apply his demoticism in the years 1920-1936, we shall see that almost all of his outlets during this period—aside from the *Odyssey*—brought him complete or partial frustration. This would seem to be one of the chief reasons determining him to make his epic poem a demotic dictionary as well as a work of art, with the unfortunate consequences that I shall treat later. Let us now, however, trace his continued linguistic involvement in some small detail, though I must omit much.

From 1920 to 1922 it was impossible for Kazantzakis to do anything, since all demotic texts were banned from the schools. The pendulum swung back slightly, however, immediately after the Asia Minor catastrophe in the autumn of 1922; it swung back completely when Venizelos resumed power in 1928. Kazantzakis was quick to respond to the various changes in climate. Even before the Plastiras *coup* in 1922, he had been negotiating with the publisher Demetrakos for a series of history textbooks for elementary school, with the stipulation that the language be demotic.[8] But his demotic was too radical even for the demoticists, and he received continual resistance from both publishers and newspaper editors. Even *Noumas* found some of his ideas on spelling unacceptable.[9]

[8] Νίκου Καζαντζάκη, Ἐπιστολὲς πρὸς τὴ Γαλάτεια, Athens, 1958, pp. 20 and 166.

[9] *Ibid*., p. 199.

In view of the climate in 1922, it would have been remarkable had Kazantzakis not been frustrated in his activities as a demoticist. But the frustrations continued even in the period 1928-1932, when conditions became extremely favorable. Not only was Venizelos back in power, as I have indicated, but Kazantzakis' friend George Papandreou held the post of Minister of Education. This comparatively favorable climate stimulated Kazantzakis to a new explosion of activity with the double aim of aiding demotic and securing himself an income. In 1930, taking advantage of the law that had been passed concerning translations of the classics, he tried to convince his friend Papandreou to award him the commission to do Plato. But luck was once more against him: "I don't have much hope for Plato," he wrote to his disciple and literary agent Pandelis Prevelakis, "now that I've read the law. The selection of the translator depends on the Academy; consequently, it is impossible for us to be chosen. And Papandreou will never be willing to put his foot down."[10]

At this same time Kazantzakis was still finding resistance to his extreme demotic, even from his own publishers. After sending the manuscript of his *History of Russian Literature* to Eleftheroudakis, for example, he confessed his fear "that he will reproach me for my language. Good God, how shameful not to be free!"[11]

Since nothing came of the hope to do Plato, he contracted with Demetrakos for a French-Greek dictionary which—as we might have guessed—never got published. This ill-fated dictionary forms a small sad story in itself,

[10] Νίκου Καζαντζάκη, *Τετρακόσια γράμματα τοῦ Καζαντζάκη στὸν Πρεβελάκη*, Athens, 1965, p. 200.
[11] *Ibid.*, p. 201.

the details of which I cannot elaborate here for lack of space. Suffice it to say that Kazantzakis' labors—the entire first half of the alphabet—went for nought.

In the years that followed, Kazantzakis did not embark on any new grandiose labor for demotic, yet the harassment caused him by his extreme demoticism continued. In 1933, still trying desperately to earn his living abroad, he experimented with a scheme whereby he would translate the best Spanish poets and write articles about Spain's cultural life. These articles would be submitted to Greek newspapers, but he would be paid by the Spanish government; the articles, in other words, would be offered free to the Greek press. As usual, he asked Prevelakis to act as his agent in Greece. "The terms are splendid," he wrote. "I don't want payments, I don't even ask that my objectionable name be printed; thus they won't even have any trouble in 'correcting' my language as much as they please."[12] Later, after a particular publisher had accepted, insisting, however, that Kazantzakis' name be used: "This bothers me, because he'll without a doubt alter the language. I'll write him to accept a pseudonym if he refuses to publish unadulterated demotic."[13] In other words, Kazantzakis insisted on preserving the integrity of his name in its relation to demotic, though his financial need obliged him to allow his articles to be "corrected."

The attitude of the newspapers was one thing; what hurt much more was criticism from supposed friends, or from the new generation of youths who, he felt, ought to have been on his side. In 1933 Kazantzakis complained to Prevelakis about a group of young authors who were preparing a manifesto "against all those who write genuine

[12] *Ibid.*, p. 356.

[13] *Ibid.*, p. 359.

demotic" ("genuine" is Kazantzakis' own term) and whose chief whipping boy was himself. "Miserable fallen generation!" is his comment.[14] As for friends, he was greatly embittered in the same year when Lefteris Alexiou, his former brother-in-law, sharply attacked his translation of Dante's *Divine Comedy* because of its *malliari* idiom. "I don't understand anything," Kazantzakis objected. "What does *malliari* mean? Rich? Where does he find the *malliarosyne*—that is, the forged, far-fetched, unintelligible word? I shudder when I see how impossible comprehension is in even such a simple, simplistic matter."[15]

In 1934 and 1935 he continued to be harassed by the newspapers. In 1935, when he was publishing a series of travel articles about Japan, he begged Prevelakis—who was again acting as his agent—to insist that the papers stop "correcting" his language. "Today they had τῆς χωνεύσεως, which is disgusting. We had agreed that they were to keep hands off."[16]

In short, the harassment and frustrations, especially in the period 1922-1936, were both too various and too continuous to leave Kazantzakis unaffected. He was getting nowhere in his battle for "genuine" (i.e., extreme) demotic; or at least the returns were completely incommensurate with the effort. But he was not affected as one might expect: he did not give in or compromise. Rather, quite the reverse: he became even more intransigent. If he could not succeed in these public ways—journalism, textbooks, dictionaries—he would succeed in a "private" way: poetry. He would make his *magnum opus*, the *Odyssey*, a textbook of demotic, a thesaurus, a dictionary. The linguistic radicalism seen in the *Odyssey* was not only a con-

[14] *Ibid.*, p. 398. [15] *Ibid.*, p. 366. [16] *Ibid.*, p. 448.

tinuation of Kazantzakis' genuine and wholly admirable love of the Greek language; it was also a compensation for his previous frustration, personal in motivation rather than artistic, and therefore in its application all too often mechanical instead of aesthetic. It was a radicalism of desperation.

I do not deny that Kazantzakis' demoticism resulted in certain improvements to the *Odyssey*, especially in the early drafts, but in general I would say that by the time he had completed the epic and poured into it all the words, not to mention the spelling, that he could use nowhere else, he still had not found a proper literary vehicle for his demoticism. This, if it came at all, was to come later, after 1940.

In any case, it is absolutely clear that for the decade 1927-1937 (roughly), Kazantzakis' demotic zeal and the writing of the *Odyssey* were inseparable components of his life. The letters written to Prevelakis while he was preparing the second draft, for instance, attest to his linguistic industriousness and enthusiasm; they also indicate his broader aims and criteria, and give examples, otherwise very rare, of some of the specific revisions he made.

The first thoughts about a second draft come from Russia in February 1929: "I'm returning through Siberia and will get off at several cities I missed on the way out. But my mind is already turned toward the *Odyssey*. I therefore have to ask you again for certain things for the *Odyssey*: (1) Words. Write me whatever new words you have found. (2) They said that the first volume of the Demotic Dictionary [i.e., the Academy's Dictionary] would be printed. Is this true? (3) Send me . . . Daskalakis' *Κυνηγὸ* [hunting terms], Drosinis' *Ψάρεμα* [fishing terms] . . .

and anything else on Greek animals and birds. . . . Love for demotic has again overcome me. Please, send whatever you think will be good for me."[17]

Subsequent letters are variations on this theme:

"I have leafed through all the Bulletins [he is speaking of the *Λεξικογραφικὸν ἀρχεῖον τῆς μέσης καὶ νέας Ἑλληνικῆς*] and have taken a good deal. Send me whatever linguistic material you have ready. . . . This draft of the *Odyssey* will be only the second; thus I have time. Perhaps I'll be in Greece during the third or fourth drafts, and then I'll resume my linguistic investigations. Maybe we can take a long trip together then, to the islands, Epirus, the Mani, Roumeli—and pillage." . . .[18]

"Do me a favor: Look through *Laographia* and find me some exorcisms and some interesting curses. Especially exorcisms against malaria." . . .[19]

"One more favor: Can you find out the demotic names for the enclosed list of birds? It's difficult, but I need them so much!" . . .[20]

"Thanks for *ζερβοδεξοχέρης*. I used it immediately."[21]

In all fairness to Kazantzakis, and in spite of what I said earlier about the lack of congruence between his linguistic program and the *Odyssey* as a work of art, there does seem to be some such congruence, especially in this second draft, when he was primarily trying to improve the verse (the later drafts being devoted to accretions of new material). Certain broader aims and criteria emerge, showing that Kazantzakis was not merely an arbitrary "collector."

He likes words, so he claims, not simply because they

[17] *Ibid.*, pp. 113-14. [18] *Ibid.*, p. 122. [19] *Ibid.*, p. 149.
[20] *Ibid.*, p. 162. [21] *Ibid.*, p. 318.

are rare, or hitherto unused in the written language, but because they are alive on the lips of the people, with all the nuances that only spoken words can develop. Thus, in criticizing the translation Prevelakis was undertaking of *Toda Raba*, Kazantzakis says he would prefer the form Moskovos to Moskovitis, because the former carries with it all the associations of the popular ballads about Daskaloyiannis' promise: Τὸ Μόσκοβο θὰ φέρω. Instead of the international term "ghetto," he would use "Ovriaki," because that is what the Jewish quarter was called in Irakleion.[22]

These general criteria may seem extremely remote from the actual poem Kazantzakis eventually produced; yet his store of living demotic expressions did enable him to transmute many of his abstractions into pictures, or at least into concretions. A good example is the revision of the opening lines of Book I, which read as follows in the first draft: *Σὰ σκότωσε τοὺς ἄνομους μνηστῆρες στὸ παλάτι. . . .* Kazantzakis replaced the abstract *σκότωσε* (killed) with the pictorial *θέρισε* (reaped, mowed down); the frequently used, colorless abstraction *ἄνομους* (unlawful) with a demotic term, abstract still, but more precise as an epithet for the suitors: *γαύρους* (haughty); the classical term *μνηστῆρες* (suitors) with the demotic "corruption" of *νέους* (youths): *νιούς*; and the noun *παλάτι* (palace) with a pictorial equivalent: *φαρδιὲς αὐλὲς* (wide courtyards). The line now reads: *Σὰ θέρισε τοὺς γαύρους νιοὺς μὲς στὶς φαρδιὲς αὐλές του. . . .*[23]

Similar revisions can be seen in three early versions of

[22] *Ibid.*, p. 148.

[23] *Ibid.*, pp. 145 and 165. We should note that *γαῦρος* is a demotic word with an impeccably ancient pedigree.

lines 4 to 6 of the Prologue, fortunately preserved for us in Kazantzakis' letters.[24] The second draft reads:

> *Καλή 'ναι ἐτούτη ἡ γῆς, ἀρέσει μας, σὰν τὸ*
> *φιλντίσι λάμπει·*
> *τί νά σκαλίσουμεν ἀπάνου της, πρὶ νὰ μᾶς πάρει*
> *ὁ Χάρος;*

The figure here—"the earth shines like ivory, what shall we carve upon it before Charon takes us?"—is trite and certainly not very indigenously Greek; it is hardly a figure that lives on the lips of the people. Thus Kazantzakis abandoned it in his first attempt at a third draft, and substituted a much more indigenous—and audacious—trope:

> *Καλή 'ναι ἐτούτη ἡ γῆς, ἀρέσει μας, σὰν τὸ*
> *σγουρὸ σταφύλι*
> *στὸν μπλάβο ἀγέρα, Θέ μου, κρέμεται, στὸν ἄνεμο*
> *κουνιέται*
> *κι ἀργάζεται μὲς στὴν ἐρμιάν, ἀργά, τὴν ἀγουρίδα μέλι.*[25]

The earth is now a curly cluster of grapes hanging in the air, swaying in the wind, and slowly "working" the individual unripe grapes into honeyed ripeness. A year and a half later, as he was strolling down the Paseo del Prado in Madrid on a bright, sunny day, he decided to change the colorless abstraction *ἄνεμος* (wind) to the rare, concrete *δρόλαπας*, a specific term for a violent, icy wind with rain, or perhaps to *καταχνιά* (mist). The concluding figure, that of working unripe grapes into honey, he abandoned completely, but in the process he introduced

[24] *Ibid.*, p. 182. [25] *Ibid.*, p. 248.

the demotic and specific τσιμπολογοῦν (peck at, nip) in place of the abstraction ἀργάζεται. This version reads:

Καλή 'ναι ἐτούτη ἡ γῆς, ἀρέσει μας, σὰν τὸ σγουρὸ
  σταφύλι
στὸν μπλάβο ἀγέρα, Θέ μου κρέμεται, στὸ δρόλαπα
  (ἢ καταχνιά;) κουνιέται
καὶ τὴν τσιμπολογοῦν τὰ πνέματα καὶ τὰ πουλιὰ
  τοῦ ἀνέμου.[26]

The definitive version is identical, retaining δρόλαπας, a word that was incomprehensible to most of his readers, instead of the familiar καταχνιά.

These examples afford only a very cursory view of the *Odyssey* as "demotic textbook." But they will give some sense, I hope, of the systematic way in which Kazantzakis introduced concretions, rare words, and outlandish metaphors into the poem—sometime to its benefit, but in the sum total, I believe, to its detriment.

When he had finished he had produced something that was extremely difficult to read, and he was forced to append a glossary of about two thousand unknown words. But even this did not solve the problem. As an example of a fully responsible reaction to the poem, I cite the critique by Elli Lambridi, a person who by and large sympathized with Kazantzakis' linguistic aims: she praises the idea of making the epic a repository for the entire demotic language, because this language is so threatened by *katharevousa*, yet demurs when it comes to the actual result. All too often the rare words are inserted for their own sake, she claims, as though Kazantzakis were writing a dictionary instead of a poem. Moreover, these words make the

[26] *Ibid.*, p. 360.

reading of the poem so difficult and cumbersome that "although I had the glossary next to me, I neglected many times to open it, with the certainty that I would not lose much if I lacked the name of a certain kind of buffalo. . . ."[27]

Other critics went much further than this and questioned the entire undertaking. One example was Markos Avyeris,[28] who asserted that as far as the rare words were concerned, they came from the "lamp," the notebook, and not from living speech; thus they were just as dead as the hated *katharevousa.* According to this view, Kazantzakis was paradoxically accomplishing precisely the opposite of what he intended.

People continued to take sides, writing long essays pro or con. But in the entire controversy, no one, so far as I know, emphasized what ought to have been most important: the fact that language cannot be discussed apart from subject matter. It is chiefly on this ground, I believe, that the *Odyssey* is a linguistic failure. Certainly a poet has the right to use difficult, even incomprehensible, words of whatever origin he chooses; certainly poetry is not common speech, even when it aspires to the quality and diction of common speech. What matters is not the type of words or grammar used, but how these elements relate to the content of the poem or novel, and how skillfully the artist has fused together expression and content so that one is unthinkable without the other. Such congruence does not exist, or exists only minimally, in the *Odyssey.* The language is rich in metaphors drawn from nature, from

[27] " 'Η 'Οδύσσεια *τοῦ* Ν. Καζαντζάκη: 'Η Μορφή *της*," Νεοελληνικὰ Γράμματα, April 15, 1939, p. 11.

[28] In " 'Η *νέα* 'Οδύσσεια," *Νέα* 'Εστία, October 1, 1939, p. 1346.

the most basic experiences of the Greek peasantry, yet at least half the poem is about Odysseus' rejection of the soil, flight from the rootedness implied in peasant life, and his final belief that nothing is real except the imaginings of the mind. Abstractions are made concrete linguistically, yet the poem treats a man who always looks beyond the concrete person or event to the abstract and metaphysical. The epic's content is generally philosophical and intellectual—not bad in itself, but bad when expressed in a language that is out-of-keeping, when a high tone clashes against a low diction. Lastly, and most comprehensively, the language, though meant to be true to the spirit of the Greek people, to express what is best in them, is employed in a poem that is removed from Greece and the Greek people, is essentially at odds with the demotic spirit, and was written by a man who, by his own confession, did not at that period "see, hear or taste the world" as a Greek does.[29]

Still, it was good that Kazantzakis wrote the *Odyssey*. Obviously, he had to write it, had to get it out of his system, and, as he would say, had to exorcise certain demons. His failure seems to have been a *felix culpa*, because something decisive happened after 1940. Perhaps the stimulus was the rigor of the German occupation, during which good and evil were all too real, and not the phantasmagoria of nothingness that Kazantzakis had made them in the *Odyssey*. The Greek people's suffering and resistance during this period gave them a unity and dignity that had been lacking in the years following the Asia Minor catastrophe. All this caused not only Kazantzakis but

[29] Νίκου Καζαντζάκη, "Ἕνα σχόλιο στὴν Ὀδύσσεια," Νέα Ἑστία, August 15, 1943, p. 1029.

many other Greek writers to change their styles and themes, to deepen their national consciousness, to reacquire knowledge of the peasant culture and thus to find their own roots. Whatever the precise reason, Kazantzakis now reimmersed himself lovingly in the Hellenic and neohellenic world. By reimmersion I mean not just something outward and superficial—such as the use of Greek characters and history in his plots—but also a deep change in attitude: a final acceptance of the natural world as both real and good; a return to earth after several decades' sojourn in the clouds of metaphysical pessimism. Most important, with this new attitude he was willing to use subject matter completely congruent with the concrete, pictorial, earthy demotic Greek that he had been championing for so many years.

It seems obvious to us, who know Kazantzakis almost exclusively through the late novels, that the modern Greeks were his proper, inevitable subject matter. Hence it is difficult for us to realize that in the thirty-three-year period between *The Masterbuilder* (1908) and the beginning of *Zorba* (1941), there is not a single page of his published imaginative writing that treats modern Greece directly or in which an actual modern Greek is allowed to speak his marvelous demotic tongue—and by "modern" I mean at least as far back as 1821.[30]

Kazantzakis' acceptances in later life were thus twofold: a new prosaic genre involving prose, and a new prosaic, earthy subject matter: the Greek people. The two went hand in hand. Gradually, very gradually, he began

[30] Kazantzakis had been experimenting in the thirties, however, with contemporary characters and settings. Strangely, most of these attempts were in French.

consciously to value the novel, to realize that the very medium he had now chosen forced him to treat his materials, modern or not, in a completely different, refreshing way. Gradually, also, he began to see the vital connection between the demotic language he had so long espoused, and the new type of peasant, agrarian material he was using. In 1948, when *Zorba* was behind him and he had begun *Christ Recrucified*, the first of the novels done in exile, he wrote to Prevelakis: "These days I have been finishing the novel I started. . . . It is contemporary, taking place in a village in Asia Minor. . . . Naturally I don't know if it is any good, but am writing it with great gusto. The novel-form offers me an outlet where I can make use of certain 'human' qualities I possess, qualities that do not find their way into poetry or drama, at least not in this manner. Good spirits, humor, ordinary 'human' everyday talk, laughter, jokes with plenty of salt, difficult concepts *formulated with peasant simplicity* [my italics] —all these were in me, and it is only in the novel that I've been able to deposit them and find relief. These things were a part of myself which had to be given expression. . . ."[31]

When Kazantzakis says "formulated with peasant simplicity," he means: conveyed in a way that preserves not just the events and facts but the flavor of Greek life. His novels do convey this flavor; that is what distinguishes them. I wish to stress my conviction that this result could not have been accomplished without his own special type of demotic. It is one of the ironies of literary history, defying all expectation, that Kazantzakis' novels "worked" when they were written in demotic and were then trans-

[31] Τετρακόσια Γράμματα, p. 592.

lated into dozens of other tongues, sometimes even at second hand, whereas when Kazantzakis himself composed directly in French, as in earlier books such as *Toda Raba*, the magical flavor failed to appear. Despite his consummate knowledge of French, he had an ear so specifically and finely tuned to demotic that in order to bring peasant speech to life he had to record it exactly as he heard it.

The later novels are their own best witnesses to Kazantzakis' final vindication of his linguistic program. Older genres and modes persisted, it is true, but all of his great gift with words, all of the knowledge and systematic collecting that provided lexical material as tools for that gift, were now, in the novels, natural collaborators in the artistic process, not arbitrary elements imposed in order to counteract the linguistic narrowness of newspapers, schoolmasters, and grammarians, nor coupled by violence with high poetic style or with abstract philosophical concerns. In the novels, the language forms a natural partnership with characterization, dialogue, narration, description. Demotic's primary virtues of concreteness and earthiness are precisely congruent with the primary virtues of these works which, as Kazantzakis himself stated, are gambols in the verdant grass of this concrete, earthy world.[32] In a sense, the novels *are* the language in which they were written. At least, all the qualities that endear them to us are most basically linguistic, the fruits of Kazantzakis' long love-affair with demotic: the metaphorical richness; the wealth of anecdote and fable, so natural and inevitable in the context of the novels (as opposed to the context of the *Odyssey*); the plenitude of detail, and especially the

[32] *Ibid.*, p. 598.

extraordinary sensitivity to the details of the natural environment; the animistic attitude toward sea, sun, stars; the combination of impassioned rhetoric with cracker-barrel pithiness. Kazantzakis gave heed, at the end of his career, to what he had done for demotic, but perhaps did not think sufficiently of what demotic had done for him. For Psycharis' beloved "Romaiika" made certain traits inevitable in the novels, and it is precisely these traits, I believe, that give the later works their value and enable us to forgive their obvious shortcomings.

After a decade of crusading demoticism, and another two decades of frustrations that drove Kazantzakis, if my analysis is correct, to impose his linguistic zeal upon the unreceptive subject matter of the *Odyssey*, he finally succeeded, in the late novels, in wedding language to material in an organic, aesthetically justifiable way. His demoticism had finally found its proper artistic embodiment.

Peter Levi, S.J.

7. Seferis' Tone of Voice

WHAT interests me about Seferis is his tone of voice in his poems.[1] It is something to do with the building up of context inside a poem, and now that we have a broad mass of his poems to live with, one can see this power of context building up in whole collections and sequences of poems and from year to year, so that one can speak of something having a resonance in the whole context of the poetry of George Seferis. I think it is important and interesting that today, for a number of reasons—some of them inside and some outside the art of poetry—a poet cannot hope to express himself fully as a human being, to make that mark or say those words we are waiting for, except in the unfolding of time: in quite a long lifework.

The building up of context is intimately linked to what a poem is. If I say: "Does the wet shipboy sleep in such a time?" the effect is not very powerful; but if I have built up an entire context of language in which I spoke almost with exaggeration about storms and the anger of heaven, and a whole dramatic context in which you feel things that have never been explicitly said, and many languages and resonances are harmoniously present to you—if in fact I am Shakespeare, then the effect of these words in the context of the play will be overwhelming. Today we are not able to command or to construct such harmonious universes; inside the small, loosely philosophic, modern poem, the power of context is not the same; the poet has to do everything, to suggest and make present his whole universe of language, in a very few

[1] The definitive version of this essay has been published in Greek under the title Ὁ *τόνος τῆς φωνῆς τοῦ Σεφέρη* (Athens, Ikaros, 1970), translated by Stratis Tsirkas and revised verbally in certain passages by George Seferis.

lines. One will understand individual poems better if one knows the whole lifework: the power of context will be greater. The way the context works in a poem largely depends on, or shows as, a tone of voice. It is the most personal thing about a poet; it can be parodied but never successfully imitated. In the case of a great poet it could not be fed into a computer because it depends on the intuitive expression in time of what is most personal in the man and on inaccessible elements that are present in the bones of the language. I do not want to say it is spiritual, because poetry is not spiritual, and language is not spiritual; at any rate we are able to study it in a material and empirical way.

Seferis' tone of voice (I am going to speak of him as if he existed only in poetry) is at once riveting to the attention. There is something very serious and very complicated about it. It obeys the important rule that poetry now has to be at least as serious, and speak of realities at least as complicated, as prose is capable of doing. Every poet must find his way of expressing, in the forms of poetry available to him, in his language as it then is, whatever he can of life: his way of animating, or rather being animated by, all the possibilities he can of his native language. Naturally not every poetic form from the past is available to a particular poet in a particular time. It is a hard task for any poet to find what forms are really available to him, let alone the question of his language. The metres of Russian poetry and the Russian language are intoxicating to listen to, but it is obvious they are not available to English poets because of the complete difference of sound values. The half-prose, half-poetic form of the travel journals of Bushō, for example, the narrow road to the far north, with its intensity and apparent simplicity, make a slightly harder case: this form is not available to English poets because of a difference in the quality of life between 18th-century Japan and the 20th century in our world. Even inside our own languages, I believe that the forms of the anonymous folksong and ballad, or the small epic, are hardly possible forms available to a modern poet either in England or in Greece. This is a difficult case; it has to do with our consciousness of the language that we were born to.

You cannot separate Seferis' tone of voice from the forms and the examples available to him. If you ask how a certain seriousness, a richness of tone that breaks through weaknesses, becomes available to a poet, there will always be an answer in terms of the progress of the poet's own work: his development of strength and harmony and economy of gesture out of the materials and instruments of his earliest poems. From that point of view Yeats is a fascinating example, and so is Cavafy. But where do the possibilities of verse come from? They belong to a particular moment in the language and a particular moment in the art of poetry. There is no poet who belongs more to his own language than Seferis; it is true of him—in a way it would not be true of Yeats—that he has created the Greek in which he speaks. But the possibilities of writing in such a tone and such a form as he has done belong to the modern movement and its masters all over Europe. No poetry could be more completely Greek than the best poetry of Seferis, and it is quite certain he has exploited veins of possibility in the Greek poetry of earlier generations that only an equally learned poet could ever rediscover, but he is a European poet in the same sense as Eliot or Quasimodo, which Yeats is not; he is a poet who became possible only because of the central traditions of European poetry in the late nineteenth century.

If modern poetry does not begin with Dante, it begins with Rimbaud. Among so much that is boyish, so many ironies and—to be honest—sentimentalities, among all the obsessive thoughts that come of such a pressure as well as such a brilliance of personality, this marvellous adolescent renewed poetry as Blake had tried and failed to renew it in England. Rimbaud created almost a new art; he is our founding father. It happened because he had too much to say. The compression and human complication of feeling is so great even in a quite simple poem by Rimbaud—say the poem about the body of the dead soldier or the great revolutionary sonnet to the French of the second Empire—that he is forced into a new technique, a really new poetic form. He drops the Comédie Française tone of voice not because it was aesthetically interesting to do so but because he was forced to; he had too much to say. His experiments are passionate, and this passion is one of many: a part of all the rest of his passions. Even now his poetry is raw as well as strong; time has not mellowed it. Because of Rimbaud it becomes suddenly possible to talk about absolutely anything in the most stinging, the most sensuous, the most serious tone at once. This is something he gave to all Europe, because the predicament he talks about is modern: it belongs to the social conditions of modern Europe, and insofar as any society reaches that same point, or any poet reaches it, he will have to learn from Rimbaud or reinvent what Rimbaud has already invented better. I think if you look at Robert Lowell's versions of Rimbaud in *Imitations* you will see that we have not got beyond the possibilities of language that Rimbaud first broke open.

There is no point in comparing stray lines of Seferis' poems with the work of individual European poets who are close to him. What is interesting is how he has reached such a point of easy compression, the kind of language he was already using with ease in *Mythistorema.* In the case of Shakespeare, Lowell, and T. S. Eliot, the first (or first published) poems are like coiled snakes, works of great technical strength that loosen up later into a full, immediate style. But there are other poets who started by publishing comparatively bad, or technically weak, poetry: Yeats, James Joyce, and Ezra Pound come into this category; so does Cavafy; and so, I think, does Tennyson. Seferis in his early poems is a curious combination of the two categories: he is surely one of those who have had to write bad poetry in order to write good; who have had first to express a fineness of reaction, a hungry sharpness of the intellectual senses, in a full, unblushing way that, under the pressure of birth, was bound to appear to the world mannered and frail. A young poet must recapitulate in himself those stages of the history of earlier poetry that have done most to make his future work possible. But the technique is modern; it is Seferis from the beginning. The imagism and the half-rhymes, and above all the governing rhythm of the voice, as early as *The Cistern* in 1932, and (except for the half-rhymes) even in his first book, *Turning Point*, in 1931, are absolutely modern and his own. It is not a phrase like *τοῦ ἔναστρου θόλου οἱ νόμοι* that determines the tone of *Erotikos Logos*; it is the description of the snakes, with the strange final rhyme (one should remember that rhyme is not a thing in itself;

it is essentially a device of rhythm) and above all the diminishing and fading of one thing into the other:

. . Μὲς στὸν καθρέφτη ἡ ἀγάπη μας, πῶς πάει καὶ
        λιγοστεύει
μέσα στὸν ὕπνο τὰ ὄνειρα, σκολειὸ τῆς λησμονιᾶς
μέσα στὰ βάθη τοῦ καιροῦ, πῶς ἡ καρδιὰ στενεύει
καὶ χάνεται στὸ λίκνισμα μιᾶς ξένης ἀγκαλιᾶς. .

Δυὸ φίδια ὡραῖα κι' ἀλαργινά, τοῦ χωρισμοῦ πλοκάμια
σέρνουνται καὶ γυρεύουνται στὴ νύχτα τῶν δεντρῶν,
γιὰ μιὰν ἀγάπη μυστικὴ σ' ἀνεύρετα θολάμια
ἀκοίμητα γυρεύουνται δὲν πίνουν καὶ δὲν τρῶν.[2]

We are not only in a world after Rimbaud; we are in a world after Jules Laforgue, and after Guillaume Apollinaire: "C'est la saison, c'est la saison, adieu vendanges! . . . Voici venir les pluies d'une patience d'ange." Modern poetry became possible not because of one man or book or language; the tradition, the open possibilities, have been modified by many comparatively obscure poets. It is the task and the lifework of every poet—and it has been a concern of Greek poets in particular: of Solomos, Seferis, and Gatsos—to know and explore every avenue of European poetry. A poet does not need to have impeccable

[2] Except for "The Cats of St. Nicholas" (see fn. 3), the Greek text of Seferis' poems is quoted either from *George Seferis: Collected Poems, 1924-1955*, trans. Edmund Keeley and Philip Sherrard, Princeton, 1967, or from *George Seferis: Three Secret Poems*, trans. Walter Kaiser, Cambridge, Mass., 1969. Both of these volumes offer facing translations in English. The Winter 1969 issue of *Agenda* (Greek Poetry Special Issue) has a relevant essay by Seferis treating the word "aesthetic," and it also offers an English version of *Three Secret Poems* by Peter Thompson under the title "Three Private Poems."

beginnings, nor does he need impeccable examples; it may be better not to have these. You may discover more from Francis Jammes or Sir John Betjeman than from a great genius like Eliot, whose lessons are all unlearnable. And just as it was the exaggeration and mannerism of art nouveau that liberated the young painters of what became the cubist movement from earlier academic conventions, so it was probably the ridiculous mannerism and aestheticism of the nineties that set free the poets of the modern movement in Europe from the dull symphonic music of the past. After all, the seeds dropped by Baudelaire were still slumbering in that ground. In the early and late poetry of Yeats and of Ezra Pound, and in a certain sense in the poetry of George Seferis, you can see all the stages in one man: first the mannerism, the dandy technique, and the confused fullness of feelings; then the liberated art, the freedom of language that could not have been built on any other beginnings.

This is not a question of particular conscious influences, or of shared subject matter. If that is what you are looking for, it is impossible to see backward through the poems of George Seferis. Poems like his could not exist if they were not opaque. The writings of a poet are not simply original achievements of an individual genius; indeed, the more the poet seems to us a genius, the more certain it is that his work began in the lives and societies and lifework of earlier poets, even if he does not know their names, even if he cannot read their languages. I am not able to suggest what foreign writings Seferis had read in which year; what interests me is his tone of voice, the intimate symptom of the man and the fine point of the style. There are certain foreign writings that influenced that tone fundamentally, whether by direct or indirect knowledge. Of these the most important is Rimbaud and the most obvious is Eliot, although my personal impression, which I suggest very diffidently, is that Eliot was himself too perfect and too peculiar a poet to have been a fruitful influence on the poetry of other writers in his own time. The same might have been true of Rimbaud in his own time.

The world of Seferis' poems is clearly stated in *Mythistorema*. In that sequence, his first masterpiece, he wrote for the first time with a brush that made clear, economic marks on the page and left no traces on the air, as Bashō puts it. The world of each poem is self-contained, but the poems belong together. In this they are very like the prose poems of Rimbaud. Rimbaud's worlds are not the same; he was a Frenchman of the 19th century even in his most intimate dreams. But they have the quality of being dreamlike and realistic at the same time (language gives a stronger sense of reality than can a dream). You are in a real world and you recognize it, but you cannot predict its rules; all the information the poet gives you is fresh to you: "J'ai embrassé l'aube d'été. Rien ne bougeait au front des palais. L'eau était morte. Les camps d'ombres ne quittaient pas la route du bois." No one can guess how the poem goes on. The coherence is nothing more than a coherent poetic context in which one phrase works on another, just as the lines of a new drawing create a new kind of space.

But one can say that Seferis' tone is more serious and more arresting than that of Rimbaud in these poems. He is more closely involved in his poem, and one has the impression it involved him from long before the point where you begin to overhear it. More important, you are involved also, nor can you ever be sure that the world is not yours: it is not quite a dream world but the real, ordinary world seen in the mirrors of a dream.

Ξύπνησα μὲ τὸ μαρμάρινο τοῦτο κεφάλι στὰ χέρια
ποὺ μοῦ ἐξαντλεῖ τοὺς ἀγκῶνες καὶ δὲν ξέρω ποῦ νὰ
τ᾽ ἀκουμπήσω.
Ἔπεφτε στὸ ὄνειρο καθὼς ἔβγαινα ἀπὸ τὸ ὄνειρο
ἔτσι ἑνώθηκε ἡ ζωή μας καὶ θὰ εἶναι πολὺ δύσκολο νὰ
ξαναχωρίσει.
—Μυθιστόρημα Γ′ (*Mythistorema*, no. 3)

This is the secret of Seferis' tone of voice: everything in his mind that is not the poem is presupposed. We are always in the center of myths that we never understand because the whole story has never been told, the implications cannot be unraveled; probably, in fact certainly, if the lines of implication in *Mythistorema* were pursued to infinity they would contradict each other. The wind can drive you mad, you wait for messengers, people go away and leave you obsessed with old ropes and cannons, someone is looking for you or you for them. Three birds of an unlikely color inscribe your fate in invisible writing on the air. This poetry is more profound than the language of existentialism because there is no question that it matters; the self of the poet has a solidity and innocence—if that is the word—of a small boy. But at the same time the self is completely adult: only that he finds himself, il se trouve, *βρίσκεται*, in the center of this poem and has the godlike power of speaking about it. The myths extend outward in every direction into the bones of the language. They are not really stories at all; they are part of our consciousness of the language. In this they are like the central situations of Graham Greene or Conan Doyle that those writers have chosen to elaborate and rationalize into novels: journeys on great trains, the hunted criminal, the hound on the moors, the fog and the violin. It is the language, I believe, that contains the thoughts we inherit.

In the poem with the epigraph *ὄνομα δ' Ὀρέστης* in *Mythistorema* (no. 16), there is a nightmare intensity of tone. The context of the poem keeps coming back at you from new directions, so that every implication leads you back into the poem. It is not exactly a poem about Orestes; the context it builds is not one you find in classical dictionaries. It has something to do with the actual words used: obviously it is the poet who suffers; Orestes is only a word for him and a word outside the poem. Everything is in the words:

Στὴ σφενδόνη, πάλι στὴ σφενδόνη, στὴ σφενδόνη,
πόσοι γύροι, πόσοι αἱμάτινοι κύκλοι, πόσες μαῦρες
σειρές· οἱ ἄνθρωποι ποὺ μὲ κοιτάζουν,
ποὺ μὲ κοιτάζαν ὅταν πάνω στὸ ἅρμα
σήκωσα τὸ χέρι λαμπρός, κι' ἀλάλαξαν.

Οἱ ἀφροὶ τῶν ἀλόγων μὲ χτυποῦν, τ' ἄλογα πότε θ' ἀποστάσουν;
Τρίζει ὁ ἄξονας, πυρώνει ὁ ἄξονας, πότε ὁ ἄξονας θ' ἀνάψει;
Πότε θὰ σπάσουν τὰ λουριά, πότε τὰ πέταλα
θὰ πατήσουν μ' ὅλο τὸ πλάτος πάνω στὸ χῶμα
πάνω στὸ μαλακὸ χορτάρι, μέσα στὶς παπαροῦνες ὅπου
τὴν ἄνοιξη μάζεψες μιὰ μαργαρίτα.
Εἶταν ὡραῖα τὰ μάτια σου μὰ δὲν ἤξερες ποῦ νὰ κοιτάξεις

δὲν ἤξερα ποῦ νὰ κοιτάξω μήτε κι' ἐγώ, χωρὶς πατρίδα
ἐγὼ ποὺ μάχομαι ἐδῶ-πέρα, πόσοι γύροι;
καὶ νιώθω τὰ γόνατα νὰ λυγίζουν πάνω στὸν ἄξονα
πάνω στὶς ρόδες πάνω στὸν ἄγριο στίβο
τὰ γόνατα λυγίζουν εὔκολα σὰν τὸ θέλουν οἱ θεοί,
κανεὶς δὲν μπορεῖ νὰ ξεφύγει, τί νὰ τὴν κάνεις τὴ δύναμη,
δὲν μπορεῖς
νὰ ξεφύγεις τὴ θάλασσα ποὺ σὲ λίκνισε καὶ ποὺ γυρεύεις
τούτη τὴν ὥρα τῆς ἀμάχης, μέσα στὴν ἀλογίσια ἀνάσα
μὲ τὰ καλάμια ποὺ τραγουδοῦσαν τὸ φθινόπωρο σὲ τρόπο
λυδικὸ
τὴ θάλασσα ποὺ δὲν μπορεῖς νὰ βρεῖς ὅσο κι' ἂν τρέχεις
ὅσο κι' ἂν γυρίζεις μπροστὰ στὶς μαῦρες Εὐμενίδες ποὺ
βαριοῦνται,
χωρὶς συχώρεση.

I am not very keen on trying to articulate what any poem is about, particularly so terrifying and moving a poem as this, but I suppose we can say loosely that this poem is about the *Εὐμενίδες*, about the presence of the Furies. In Seferis' poetry the furies are never far away. His mythology is coherent, as Professor Keeley has pointed out,[3] but it cannot be catalogued. The furies are present because they are irreducibly present in the language: they are in those thoughts and feelings which are the innermost marrow of Seferis' Greek, and this is what builds up the context: this is the poem, this is where we are, *ἐδῶ βρισκόμαστε*. In a work of mature power like *Three Secret Poems*, the appearance of Hekate is unannounced. There

[3] In "Seferis and the 'Mythical Method,'" *Comparative Literature Studies* (June 1969).

is no external scaffolding; the only myth is the implicit meanings of the words which we sense without articulating:

Στὴ ζεστὴ νύχτα
ἡ μαραμένη ἱέρεια τῆς Ἑκάτης
μὲ γυμνωμένα στήθη ψηλὰ στὸ δῶμα
παρακαλᾶ μιὰ τεχνητὴ πανσέληνο, καθὼς
δυὸ ἀνήλικες δοῦλες ποὺ χασμουριοῦνται
ἀναδεύουν σὲ μπακιρένια χύτρα
ἀρωματισμένες φαρμακεῖες.
Αὔριο θὰ χορτάσουν ὅσοι ἀγαποῦν τὰ μυρωδικά.
(III, 5)

The freedom of rhythm in these late poems, and their strongly marked variety of tone within a smaller compass than ever, tempt the reader not to notice how powerful they are. I cannot find anything like them in other European poetry except perhaps in Quasimodo and Montale, and, at an even greater distance, in Lorca. There is no analogy in Russian or in German since Mandelstam and Trakl. English poetry has gone off on its own at present, in a different direction. In France, Eluard before his death and Aragon for many years struggled to simplify their talent, or—as Eliot said of certain changes in Keats that were in fact changes for the worse—to unify their sensibility. Seferis has never done that. What a poet works in is language, and you cannot unify the sensibility of the English or the Greek language. One might pick on the words

ἀγάπησα κάποιους ἀνθρώπους ἄγνωστους
ἀπαντημένους ξαφνικὰ στὸ ἔβγα τῆς μέρας,

μονολογώντας σὰν καπετάνιοι βουλιαγμένης ἀρμάδας,
σημάδια πῶς ὁ κόσμος εἶναι μεγάλος.

—Ἕνας Λόγος γιὰ τὸ Καλοκαίρι
("A Word for Summer")

That is the tone of Seferis' early middle years (autumn 1936) and of perhaps his strongest personal poems. Later a very black lamenting note entered his voice in the poems of the war; it was the first time he had spoken so directly about public themes, and the way he did so was painful and direct. Yet the texture of the poems, shocking as it still is, has the same density and energy as his poems always had:

Ποιὸς *θέλει τώρα νὰ λουστεῖ στὰ νερὰ τοῦ* Πρωτέα;
Τὴ *μεταμόρφωση τὴ γυρέψαμε στὰ νιάτα μας*
μὲ πόθους ποὺ ἔπαιζαν σὰν τὰ μεγάλα ψάρια
σὲ πέλαγα ποὺ φύραναν ξαφνικά·
πιστεύαμε στὴν παντοδυναμία τοῦ κορμιοῦ.
Καὶ *τώρα βγῆκε τὸ νέο φεγγάρι ἀγκαλιασμένο*
μὲ τὸ παλιό· μὲ τ' ὄμορφο νησὶ ματώνοντας
λαβωμένο· τὸ ἤρεμο νησί, τὸ δυνατὸ νησί, τὸ ἀθῶο.
Καὶ *τὰ κορμιὰ σὰν τσακισμένα κλαδιὰ*
καὶ σὰν ξεριζωμένες ρίζες.

—Μέρες τοῦ Ἰουνίου '41
("Days of June '41")

The ghastly double image of the bodies needs no comment. There is hardly anything else in European poetry at that time to put beside these lines, perhaps only another poem of defeat, the Fugue for a barrel-organ in Aragon's wartime collection, *Le Crève-cœur*.

The grief and the condemnation that Seferis has on very few occasions expressed in his poems have the force of powerful art: his poetry is an organ, not a flute. The rage and the despair of certain poems are Miltonic, but it is never like the anger of Brecht, a unified sensibility. Seferis is in the language like an alchemist among potions; however black his theme and his pronouncement, there are always other elements in the darkness, the solution is never resolved. That is because his myth is equivalent to the Greek language itself, and the force of his despair, whether it is public or personal, has the inevitability of something that belongs to the language itself: it is ourselves, we cannot alter it. I hope I am not speaking mystically about this: unless I am mistaken, as a foreigner may be, it is an objective matter. It is simply that Seferis is so true to the language he uses, his tone is so true to it, that the moral and aesthetic values that truly belong to the language are present to the reader in his use of it, in the same inevitable way as certain values are present in the *Iliad* almost in spite of the epic form of the poem. This is a mark of absolutely genuine language; it is often found in popular art, but I believe seldom in European poetry. Eliot imposes values of his own, even in the *Four Quartets*. The aesthetic and social values of Yeats' poetry are often flatly contrary to the sense of the English language. Seferis' tone of voice has a complicated purity about it that depends on his language always being quite genuine; everything in the poem, and the increasing weight of context that bears on each fresh line as you hear it, rings completely true. The aspiration to write in such a way began with Wordsworth and Burns and Solomos; it cannot be achieved except by a learned poetry. There is a level at which the language of Seferis is simple, but with the apparent simplicity of ballads and chronicles, which is not simple at all:

> Ἡ *θάλασσα· πῶς ἔγινε ἔτσι ἡ θάλασσα;*
> Ἄ*ργησα χρόνια στὰ βουνά·*
> *μὲ τύφλωσαν οἱ πυγολαμπίδες.*

The syntax of these lines from *Three Secret Poems*, II, 4—and of the volume generally—is that of monologue: the energy is an energy of tone and rhythm. The rhythm does its work in your mind as much by context and succession as the images. If there is a European analogy that is any use at all it is Jules Laforgue; but in these poems we are not dealing with a young poet. By this time most of what Seferis has learned, most of the possibilities open to him, are the product of his own lifework; he has opened these possibilities himself. It is true that certain poets create the future of their own poetry, and there are poets who reduce themselves to silence. No one could have arrived immediately at the late work of Shakespeare; it was only his own early work that made his late plays possible. Even though he was stimulated at the end of his life by much lesser men, the opportunities he himself had created in a full lifework made the stimulus fruitful. Eliot, on the other hand, seems to have reduced himself to a kind of silence by a technical as well as a spiritual logic. Nor is it easy to believe that Dante, had he lived, could have gone on writing. It has something to do with language and literary form rather than subject matter, I think, and probably a function of the relation of a writer to his own society and to the rest of the human race in his writing.

At least that would explain in English the drying up of Matthew Arnold and the prolific fruitfulness of Thomas Hardy and John Clare.

Such a relationship is deeply buried in poetry, near the roots. The general sense of Seferis' poetry is tragic, but it no more excludes his own people than the work of Shakespeare. A poet identifies with a wide range of humanity and reality by his identification with the breadth of his native language. In English the modern example is James Joyce. The economy and the intense power of Seferis' style as it has developed have limited his range. He is not a writer of Shakespearean comedies or of works like *Ulysses*, nor would that have been possible for a Greek writer of his generation; but the substance of breadth is there, and his writing has not ceased to develop, even at this time. There is a generosity of spirit in his poems that, if I may say so, is very Greek, even when his voice is one of black lamentation:

> Τὸν καιρὸ τῆς μεγάλης στέγνιας,
> —σαράντα χρόνια ἀναβροχιὰ—
> ρημάχτηκε ὅλο τὸ νησί·
> πέθαινε ὁ κόσμος καὶ γεννιούνταν φίδια.[4]

This is from "The Cats of St. Nicholas," a poem of despair and the acceptance of despair that was written in 1969. As far as I know, it is the most recent work Seferis has finished. Like the famous poem about the mules, this is about real events and what they mean. The epigraph is from Aeschylus and refers to the Furies. The scene is set

[4] The Greek text is taken from Δεκαοχτὼ Κείμενα (*Eighteen Texts*), Athens, 1970, pp. 14-15. An English translation by Edmund Keeley appeared in *Encounter* (July 1969), pp. 3-4, and in *Eighteen Texts*, Cambridge, Mass., 1972.

on a ship passing that headland in Cyprus where cats were once kept at a monastery to fight against a plague of snakes. I would like to conclude everything I have had to say with the end of this constricted, but I believe great, poem.

"Τὸν καιρὸ τῆς μεγάλης στέγνιας,
—σαράντα χρόνια ἀναβροχιὰ—
ρημάχτηκε ὅλο τὸ νησί·
πέθαινε ὁ κόσμος καὶ γεννιούνταν φίδια.
Μιλλιούνια φίδια τοῦτο τ' ἀκρωτήρι,
χοντρὰ σὰν τὸ ποδάρι ἀνθρώπου
καὶ φαρμακερά.
Τὸ μοναστήρι τ' ἄη Νικόλα τό εἶχαν τότε
Ἁγιοβασιλεῖτες καλογέροι
κι' οὔτε μπορούσαν νὰ δουλέψουν τὰ χωράφια
κι' οὔτε νὰ βγάλουν τὰ κοπάδια στὴ βοσκή·
τοὺς ἔσωσαν οἱ γάτες ποὺ ἀναθρέφαν.
Τὴν κάθε αὐγὴ χτυποῦσε μιὰ καμπάνα
καὶ ξεκινούσαν τσοῦρμο γιὰ τὴ μάχη.
Ὅλη μέρα χτυπιούνταν ὣς τὴν ὥρα
ποὺ σήμαιναν τὸ βραδυνὸ ταγίνι.
Ἀπόδειπνα πάλι ἡ καμπάνα
καὶ βγαίναν γιὰ τὸν πόλεμο τῆς νύχτας.
Εἴτανε θαῦμα νὰ τὶς βλέπεις, λένε,
ἄλλη κουτσή, κι' ἄλλη στραβή, τὴν ἄλλη
χωρὶς μύτη, χωρὶς αὐτί, προβιὰ κουρέλι.
Ἔτσι μὲ τέσσερις καμπάνες τὴν ἡμέρα
πέρασαν μῆνες, χρόνια, καιροὶ κι' ἄλλοι καιροί.
Ἄγρια πεισματικὲς καὶ πάντα λαβωμένες
ξολόθρεψαν τὰ φίδια μὰ στὸ τέλος
χαθήκανε· δὲν ἄντεξαν τόσο φαρμάκι.

Ὡσὰν καράβι καταποντισμένο
τίποτε δὲν ἀφήσαν στὸν ἀφρὸ
μήτε νιαούρισμα, μήτε καμπάνα.
Γραμμή!
Τί *νὰ σοῦ κάνουν οἱ ταλαίπωρες*
παλεύοντας καὶ πίνοντας μέρα καὶ νύχτα
τὸ αἷμα τὸ φαρμακερὸ τῶν ἑρπετῶν.
Αἰῶνες *φαρμάκι· γενιὲς φαρμάκι*".
"Γραμμή!" *ἀντιλάλησε ἀδιάφορος ὁ τιμονιέρης.*

Stavros Deligiorgis

8. *Elytis' Brecht*

and

Hadzidakis' Pirandello

"I went down to the Piraeus
yesterday to observe the
celebrations . . . of the new
goddess from Thrace . . ."—Socrates

I

FOREIGNNESS in art has never been foreign to the Greeks. The ancient Greeks heard it in the chorus of the Homeric hymn to Apollo,[1] and they implied it whenever they used the term ξένον (*xenon*) as an honorific in an *ekphrasis*. The fictive "educations" of numberless wise Greeks among Indians, Egyptians, and near-Easterners,[2] Odysseus' listening to new songs with every new adventure away from his home,[3] and the application of terms suggestive of foreignness in ancient musical theory,[4] invite a reconsideration of those onesided histories that show a Greece that never was. It would be safer, in fact, to think

[1] *Homeri opera*, Thomas W. Allen, ed., Oxford, 1959, vol. v, hymn III, ll. 162-64, and *apparatus criticus*. Allen, through his choice of κρεμβαλιαστύν (*krembaliastyn*), stresses the sound of castanet accompaniment. The French editor Jean Humbert in his *Homère: Hymnes* (in the "Budé" series), Paris, 1959, pp. 85-86, ll. 162-64, note 1, by preferring βαμβαλιαστύν (*bambaliastyn*)—which is attested by some manuscripts—stresses the idea of glossolalia and, thus, the incomprehensibility of foreign speech. See his "Un mot nouveau (?): *bambaliastýs," Mélanges offerts a A. M. Desrousseaux*, Paris, 1937, pp. 225-28.

[2] Pythagoras and Plato visited Egypt; Apollonius of Tyana went to Egypt and India. There is no end to the list. The data are presented and commented in Hermann Diels' *Die Fragmente der Vorsokratiker*, Walther Kranz, ed., 5th ed., 3 vols., Berlin, 1934-1937.

[3] *Od.* 8.250-53 (the Phaeacians); *Od.* 10.221 (Circe); *Od.* 12.192-93 (the Sirens).

[4] E.g., Phrygian, Lydian, Mixo-Lydian, etc.

of Greece as an area where things have entered freely, and where the process of assimilation has made the nod of recognition more frequent than the shock of surprise.

The earliest organized introduction of foreign linguistic and cultural materials into Greek was meant for the use of Hellenized Jews, not Greeks.[5] When these materials began to be used by Greeks in the Christian liturgy, however, their value was thought to be primarily doctrinal and only secondarily aesthetic. Nevertheless, parts of the Septuagint, or rather aspects of it, did beget Pisidis' Ἑξαήμερον (*Hexahemeron*), Elytis' Ἕξη καὶ μία τύψεις γιὰ τὸν οὐρανὸ (*Six and One Regrets for the Sky*), and Seferis' "translations" of the *Song of Songs* (ᾎσμα ᾀσμάτων) and the *Apocalypse*. On the level of popular penetration, the case of the Septuagint can be compared only to the penetration of translations in the dramatic mode: while a foreign play may not generate another play in its image, parts from it may have a separate and long career primarily because of the relationship that its translator makes possible between the text and its audiences.

The case of the Septuagint is, also, the last one that may be understood as "translation" in the strict sense of the word, since, as we survey the course of Greek literary culture, we find the Cypriot renditions of Petrarch's sonnets, the chivalric romances, the Μισμαγιές (*Mismagies*) of Rhegas, and Gatsos' Lorca, to be translations as much of

[5] The amount of scholarship on the cultural and linguistic exchanges between the Greek and the Semitic peoples before Homer and the Septuagint is growing at a fast pace. Two titles will suffice: Cyrus Gordon's *Before the Bible; the Common Background of the Greek and Hebrew Civilizations*, New York, 1962, and M. C. Astour's *Hellenosemitica; an Ethnic and Cultural Study in West Semitic Impact on Mycenaean Greece*, Leiden, 1965.

the spirit as of the letter of the originals behind them. Yet the term "translation" must be retained, on the one hand because of its connotative range and the variety of activities it can cover; on the other, strange as it may sound, because of its normative fixity, and the fact that it can be one of the few measures of achievement beyond the narrowly circumscribed boundaries of "fidelity." A discussion, therefore, of foreign influences in the modern period should begin with a scrutiny of the act of translation and *its* final foreignness. This can be done, however, only by looking at it against the native cultural backdrop. In simpler terms, we must keep asking questions such as these: what native equivalents to the foreign elements are being evoked in the work of the translator, or the mind of the audience? And, conversely, what are the new phenomena, the new things in the text, or in its performance, in the context of the new culture, and what happens to them? Odysseus Elytis' four songs for Brecht's *Caucasian Chalk Circle* and Manos Hadzidakis' three songs for Pirandello's *Tonight We Improvise* could be good sources for answers to these questions.

First, let us consider Elytis' relationships to his Brecht.[6]

[6] The text of this play is relatively stable. I use Bertolt Brecht, *Die kaukasische Kreidekreis*, Berlin, 1964. "Da machte der liebe sich auf" is on p. 68; "Vier Generale" is on pp. 40-41; "Da dich keiner nehmen will" is on p. 59; "Tief ist der Abgrund" is on p. 62; and "Dein Vater" is on p. 63. Translations will be found in *Parables for the Theater: Two Plays by Bertolt Brecht* (The Good Woman of Setzuan *and* The Caucasian Chalk Circle), revised English versions by Eric Bentley, Minneapolis, 1965. "And the lover started to leave" is on pp. 134-35; "Four Generals" is on p. 120; "Since no one else will take you" is on p. 128; "Deep is the abyss" is on p. 130; and "Your father" is on p. 131. Elytis' translations, set to music by Manos Hadzidakis, can be found on

The song with the fewest differences from the original German is a *chanson de toile*—literally, a weaving song—which the heroine of Brecht's play sings at the loom (Appendix I). In the context of her personal story, her advice for survival through avoidance of extremism amounts to a very clear anticipation of the hero's return. The only variance from Brecht is that in the Greek we do not hear of the rallying around the flag where safety is.

Another early song in the play is a child's piece that the heroine, Grushe, sings to her charge as she walks away from the occupied capital (Appendix II). The first stanza is about four inept generals who are good for nothing. The second stanza, in contradistinction to the first, presents "our man Sosso Robakidse," who is good at everything. Elytis' Greek omits the feats of the latter, and it is a good decision, I think. It de-domesticates the conclusion and, through reiteration, it intensifies the ridicule leveled at the militarists of the first stanza. We may say, also, that the translator saved the Greek actress some fairly forbidding Caucasian tongue-twisting sibilants. By varying the sense of the first stanza, instead of introducing antipodal material in the original German, Elytis gives a reinforced impression of the heroine as a deliberate commentator on the evils that beset her existence and her love.

Another piece that is fairly close to the German in tone and language is the one that Grushe sings to the child when she makes up her mind to keep him for good (Appendix III). It is a piece that is in perfect agreement with the play, and could perhaps be called emblematic of all of

---

Τέσσερα τραγούδια τοῦ Ὀδυσσέα Ἐλύτη ἀπὸ τὸν Κύκλο μὲ τὴν Κιμωλία (Tessera tragoudia tou Odyssea Elyti apo ton Kyklo me tin Kimolia), a 45 r.p.m. Fidelity record, EP8902.

Brecht, especially his persistent inversions of established values.

There is, finally, a lullaby in the Greek version of the play that could have been written by Brecht but that, really, never was (Appendix IV). "Once upon a time . . ." sounds like a telescoping of several songs in the *Chalk Circle*, but the German original just is not there. This case of an original that did not quite make it to its translation, as Borges would have said[7]—a case in which Elytis goes beyond the letter of the text to a non-existent but extremely probable prototype—illustrates his sensitivity to the spirit of the German play.

We might ask, at this point, the second part of an earlier question: what are the relationships that these four poems —considered as Greek poems—have to things Greek? The weaving song that we examined first would have a good number of familiar elements about it, and also some intriguing, but not surprising, combinations of traditional elements. To begin with, there are countless metrical gnomic expressions in classical and modern Greek folklore that propound moderation. The new elements are, however, that the person being counselled is not present, and that the advice is made part of a weaving song. From Penelope, to the Virgin Mary of the Greek Protevangelium Iacobi, and Argyris Eftaliotis' "Song of the Loom"— which is so well known in modern Greece that it is synonymous with Sophia Vembo, who made it famous—the Greeks have never lost touch with the theme of return

[7] Jorge Luis Borges, *Other Inquisitions: 1937-1952,* R. L. C. Simms, trans., Intr. by J. E. Irby, New York, 1966, p. 146; speaking of W. Beckford's *Vathek*, composed in French in 1782, then translated into English in 1785.

and reunion (*nostos*) that is presented from the point of view of the tested, but faithful, heroine.[8]

Analogues to the anti-militaristic ditty are so numerous in the Greek liberal tradition—which, incidentally, Brecht knew and profoundly appreciated[9]—that a simple enumeration will have to begin with Aristophanes' antecedents and come down the ages to Souris and Kazantzakis.

The adoption song, in which the child is called an orphan, even though his mother is alive and worrying about her wardrobe, contains references to baptism. It is by necessity a wartime baptism, and as such is the exact opposite of the usual peaceful celebration that an audience normally expects. In Greek folklore the christening days are so crucial to the child that, aside from the ordinary festivities, oracular rituals are observed that are thought to govern the child's entire life. For Brecht, the ritual in vicissitude is in direct opposition to the sumptuousness and the pomp of the beginning of the play with which the court goes to mass as the populace bows and prostrates itself. For a Greek audience (though it senses an aftertaste of Byzantinism to all monarchic religious fanfare), the rigors of rituals in adversity, the rejection of past riches, the icy water and the wilderness bring up visions of an in-

[8] Western medieval weaving songs are traced to the Greek apocryphal gospels by C. B. Lewis in "The Origin of the Weaving Songs," *PMLA*, 37 (1932), 141-81. Argyris Eftaliotis' "Tragoudi tou argaliou" is printed in his Ἅπαντα (*Works*), ed. by G. Valetas, Athens, 1952, vol. 1, p. 54; the song was first published in Ἑστία (*Estia*), 1890a, p. 94.

[9] For recent work in this area see Hans Mayer, *Bertolt Brecht und die Tradition*, Pfullingen, 1961; Peter Witzmann, *Antike Tradition im Werk Bertolt Brechts*, Berlin, 1964; and Max Spalter's *Brecht's Tradition*, Baltimore, 1967.

auspicious sequel. The song contains a displacement of traditional association and, in this respect, is akin to the lullaby that is not there in the German.

Some of the materials for the lullaby, to be sure, we will find divided between two songs that deal, independently of one another, with the subject of hunger and ignominious parentage. The main thrust of the song, however, is in the way in which the child is addressed. In the folk traditions that we all know, every sleeping infant is a prince; in this case prince Michael is an ordinary infant, and the song intended to lull him—unlike the song that ordinary infants hear—is about his present destitution and, instead of the promises of affluence implied by such staples as "*Κοιμήσου καὶ παράγγειλα στὴν* Πόλι *τὰ προικιά σου*" (Sleep; I have ordered your dowry at Constantinople),[10] he hears about hopes of a plain good mother. The song may be true to no particular original lyrics, but it is true to the play, and, even more importantly, true to Elytis' own verse, which—already before the Second World War—innovated by inverting conventional usage and representation.[11] Elytis' lullaby is an illustration of the process of literary confrontation and interpenetration: paradoxical as it may sound, the moral seems to be that nothing gets anywhere unless a good part of it is already there. Information engineers call this "anticipatory pat-

[10] For variants to this traditional theme of grandeur see Ἑλλη-*νικὰ δημοτικὰ τραγούδια* (*Greek Folk Songs*), D. Petropoulos, ed., Athens, 1959, Vol. II, pp. 145-47.

[11] See, e.g., his "Ἡ *τρελλὴ ροδιά*," "Ἡ *γέννησι τῆς μέρας*" etc., in H. N. Apostolides' Ἀνθολογία *1708-1952* (*Anthology, 1708-1952*), Athens, 1954, pp. 176, 178, and notes on p. 836. The poems appeared originally in Τὰ Νέα *Γράμματα*, 1939.

terning"; games theorists call it "set outguessing"; aestheticians call it "artistic preparedness."

II

Unless we conceive of the formula of interaction in the most flexible terms—even by having to stretch our methodological outlook—we will not be able to accommodate cases like Pirandello, who, through a play of his, occasioned the creation of three widely circulated and popular songs but did so by providing the context rather than the text for them.[12] The sung parts of *Questa sera si recita a soggetto* (Tonight We Improvise; in Greek: Ἀπόψε αὐτοσχεδιάζουμε) are actually processional hymns for a full-blown Sicilian litany, and parodied snatches from Bizet and Verdi! In the Greek a good deal of this had to go. One of the reasons is that Pirandello was flaunting his problem play in the face of the frozen histrionics of the Italian dramatic traditions that parallel the Greek only in part.

The three songs in the Greek version of the play are divided between a spectral *chanteuse*, who is supposed to sing "lugubremente le parole del jazz" in a cabaret, and the moribund Mommina, who is supposed to sing the famous (and male) "Leonora, addio" from *Il Trovatore*.[13]

[12] The collected plays are in two volumes published under the general title *Maschere Nude*, Milano, 1958; "Questa sera si recita a soggetto" is in the first volume, pp. 221-311. For an English version see Samuel Putnam, trans., *Tonight We Improvise*, New York, 1932. Manos Hadzidakis' songs discussed here are on Ἀπόψε αὐτοσχεδιάζουμε (Tonight We Improvise), a 45 r.p.m. Columbia record, SEGG 2599.

[13] "Jazz": "Questa sera . . . ," p. 249; "Il Trovatore": *ibid.*, pp. 307-10.

The Greek, needless to say, is faithful to Pirandello's instructions on the point of "lugubremente," but, beyond this, there is neither jazz nor opera. Manos Hadzidakis, who composed for Dimitri Myrat's staging, unlike Manolis Hiotis, who a few years before had introduced syncopation in the native bouzouki music,[14] decided to keep the melody true to the Sicilian spirit of the play, and the lyrics true to his personal imagism. In retrospect, his incidental pieces for *Tonight We Improvise* have the proper mixture of the tarantella and a near-eastern, languorous rhythm to suggest precisely what Pirandello meant by the cabaret as opposed to the church chant. The relationships, however, that the songs have to the play—and they are functional relationships—cannot be deduced from their "content"; they must be inferred from their position in the play, their relationships to each other, and their tone.

For Mommina—one of the principal female roles in Ἀπόψε *αὐτοσχεδιάζουμε* (*Tonight We Improvise*)—Hadzidakis wrote a metamorphic piece. It is a soliloquy that is sung, *in extremis*, by the imprisoned heroine (Appendix v). Actually, the prison is supposed to be make-believe, and the death agony just acting. Pirandello's prison aria from *Il Trovatore* is replaced by Hadzidakis' "'Η Πέτρα" ("Stone"), in which the heroine goes beyond the idea of confinement and limitation to the idea of trans-

[14] For the background of these developments in popular compostions see p. 10 of A. A. Fatouros' "'Night Without Moon': A Glimpse of the Rebetika," an unpublished mimeographed article, read at the MGSA seminar of the Modern Language Association in New York (Seminar 51: "The Greek Folksong and Its Contributions to Nineteenth and Twentieth-Century Literature"), 27 December, 1970.

formation: stone is first equated with death, then with life, and then it is made the source of beauty in the form of white jasmine in bloom. Stone "breaks" the human voice, as the song says, and as such is an emblem of frustrated communication in general, and of the play in particular, which refuses to go as all plays go. Of course, there is ambiguity about the identity of the speaker after one point, when the "I" stands for a supra-personal and cosmic cry or voice, not for the utterer of the voice. This reification is topped by an appeal to the elements of wine and fire as the only ones that will destroy the pain of the speaker. It is a poem of ultimate conditions, and we may sense that Mommina plays a dirty trick on her fellow "actors" when she turns the aging and imprisonment that they impose on her into the sacrificial self-immurement and transfiguration that allows the play to end; but this we owe as much to Hadzidakis as to Pirandello, who just wanted her to die, first like a Verdi heroine who never made it, and then like someone meant to die for good.

"*Φέρτε μου ἕνα μαντολίνο*" ("Bring me a mandolin") is another metamorphic poem (Appendix VI). Its lines turn a popular musical instrument into a medium that makes one's innermost self visible. Next comes a transformation into a flower and then annihilation.[15] This may happen because someone beloved asks two questions only

[15] The antiquity of the *topos* of disappearance is impressive. It is usually combined with the motifs of love, music, and sadness. See, for instance, the story of Canens in Ovid's *Metamorphoses*, 14.320; Echo in Longus' *Daphnis and Chloe*, 3.23; perhaps Orpheus too, since, following his dismemberment, it was the landing of his head on Lesbos that was believed to have made that island musical (Virgil, *Georgics*, 4.525).

about natural and ritual cycles in time. He forgets to consider the time in which unrepeatable events (such as love) also happen.

Life, grief, identity—is what the songs are all about. In "Ὁ Ταχυδρόμος" ("The Mailman") these themes reappear multiplied but unmutated (Appendix VII). The messenger would have been the receiver of a promised message; now that he is dead the message can neither be sent nor received, and in his death his beloved dies also, since the two are one, sender and receiver, female and male "together." "The Mandolin" and "The Mailman" are sung by the *chanteuse* in the cabaret, and illustrate directly the drama of the tenuous communication between the creator and his creation, between the director and his actors, and that between the actors and their roles as characters, all three of which alternate as the subject of the play. In the plot itself, the elder lover of the *chanteuse*, a married man with a family, tries to announce his stabbing to his own home but cannot make himself heard above the arias from *Carmen* sung during a noisy gathering. When he does get to saying what he wanted to announce, he has to submit to suffering once more and then die that his fellow actors and the "director" may be satisfied. In one song Hadzidakis conflates petrified Niobe, the *planctus* of the masterbuilder's wife about to be walled up, and an almost Shakespearean, but tragic, personification of Wall with a will and a love of its own. In the other two he gives us two *heroides*, victimized, lovelorn and lonely, the one like Hyacinthus and Narcissus turning into a flower, the other a ἡρωὶς unable to send her epistle to her young lover who, like a mythological dead ἥρως, helps nature make music.

III

We must note that it was Hadzidakis who set to music Elytis' lyrics for Brecht. Dissimilar though Elytis and Hadzidakis may be, in these particular tasks at least we observe Elytis bringing out the popular element in cultural self-awareness without sentimentalizing, and Hadzidakis, in his own texts, stressing the existential problems of the Mediterranean man without archaizing or classicizing. This does not seem like a mean accomplishment when, for at least one hundred years, the Greeks of the cities have been feeding on propriety, the unities, sweetness ("γλυκύτης"), and sublimity under a host of guileful guises: operas, operettas, musicals, variety shows, popular "comic idylls," and, more recently, the movies. McLuhan would have called them all hot styles. The only form that stayed cool, it seems, was Karaghiozis, the shadow puppet shows for young and old in Greece. What we would now consider modern—and either Brechtian or Pirandellesque—such as an open structure, social consciousness, and psychological definition (regardless of the dictates of learned "poetics"), is there in Karaghiozis' mixed styles, but also in Lucian's satiric explorations, and in Aristophanes' indignant explosions.[16]

There are several morals for us to live with now. The

[16] For the relevance of Karaghiozis to a discussion of such polished names as Aristophanes, Lucian, Brecht, and Pirandello, consult the last chapters of C. H. Whitman's *Aristophanes and the Comic Hero,* Cambridge, Mass., 1964. Materials on Karaghiozis are currently being collected by Mr. Mario Rinvolucri for the Milman Parry Institute of Oral Literature at Harvard University. For details, see the *Modern Greek Studies Association Bulletin*, vol. 1, no. 2 (December 1969), p. 3.

indices to the "reception" of a literary phenomenon in a foreign country must go beyond "number of editions," the importance of translators, and the amount and quality of scholarship generated. The kind of translation, the relationship to cognate native phenomena, and, even, the presence of special conditions (classes of people denied access to a certain theater; bouzouki music not played by certain radio stations) seem like the obvious complements to the classical comparatist approach. But behind these there is another *desideratum*: a deep ethnographic acquaintance with the people receiving the *xenoi*; in most cases the latter prove to have always been there under some form or another, quite a bit like the "lamed vovniks" in our midst, the strange good men who prevent the world from blowing up.

Appendix

I

Τὴν ὥρα ποὺ ὁ λεβέντης στὸν πόλεμο κινοῦσε
Ἡ ἀγαπημένη του ἔκλαιγε καὶ τὸν παρακαλοῦσε:
Μακρυὰ στὴν μάχη σὰν βρεθεῖς, καλέ μου, ἔχε τὸν νοῦ σου·
Φυλάξου ἀπὸ τὴν μάνητα, κι' ἀπ' τὸ σπαθὶ τ' ὀχτροῦ σου.
Μπροστὰ πολὺ μὴν προχωρεῖς, πίσω μὴν ἀπομένεις:
Μπροστὰ φωτιά, πίσω φωτιά, καταμεσὶς νὰ μένεις.
Μονάχα ξέρει ὁ μεσιανὸς νὰ τρέξει, νὰ πηδήξει·
Αὐτὸς μονάχα σπίτι του μιὰ μέρα θὰ γυρίσει.

Μάνος Χατζιδάκις, Τέσσερα τραγούδια τοῦ 'Οδυσσέα 'Ελύτη ἀπὸ τὸν "Κύκλο μὲ τὴν Κιμωλία," (Manos Hadzidakis, *Tessera Tragoudia tou Odyssea Elyti Apo ton* "Kyklo me tin kimolia"), Fidelity, EP 8902. [Record]

Da machte der Liebe sich auf, zu gehen
Da lief di Anverlobte bettelnd ihm nach
Bettelnd und weinend, weinend und belehrend:
Liebster mein, Liebster mein
Wenn du nun ziehst in den Krieg
Wenn du nun fichtst gegen die Feinde
Stürz dich nicht vor den Krieg
Und fahr nicht hinter dem Krieg
Vorne ist ein rotes Feuer
Hinten ist roter Rauch.
Halt dich in des Krieges Mitten
Halt dich an den Fahnenträger.
Die ersten sterben immer
Die letzten werden auch getroffen
Die in der Mitten kommen nach Haus.

From: Bertolt Brecht, *Der kaukasische Kreidekreis,* Berlin, 1964, p. 68.

And the lover started to leave
And his betrothed ran pleading after him
Pleading and weeping, weeping and teaching:
"Dearest mine, dearest mine
When you go to war as now you do
When you fight the foe as soon you will
Don't lead with the front line
And don't push with the rear line
At the front is red fire
In the rear is red smoke
Stay in the war's center
Stay near the standard bearer
The first always die
The last are also hit
Those in the center come home."

From: Eric Bentley, trans., *Parables for the Theater: Two Plays by Bertolt Brecht*, Minneapolis, 1965, pp. 134-35.

II

Τέσσερεις στρατηγοὶ κινᾶν καὶ πᾶν,
Γιὰ πόλεμο στὸ μακρυνὸ τὸ Ἰράν.
Ὁ πρῶτος ἀπὸ πόλεμο δὲν κάτεχε,
Ὁ δεύτερος στὶς κακουχιὲς δὲν ἄντεχε,
Ὁ τρίτος ἦταν ὑποκείμενο γελοῖο,
Κι' ὁ τέταρτος φοβότανε τὸ κρύο.

Τέσσερεις στρατηγοὶ κινᾶν καὶ πᾶν,
Ἀλλὰ δὲν φτάνουνε ποτὲ στὸ Ἰράν.

Μάνος Χατζιδάκις, *Τέσσερα τραγούδια τοῦ Ὀδυσσέα Ἐλύτη*

ἀπὸ τὸν "Κύκλο μὲ τὴν Κιμωλία," (Manos Hadzidakis, *op.cit.*)

Vier Generäle
Zogen nach Iran.
Der erste führte keinen Krieg
Der zweite hatte keinen Sieg
Dem dritten war das Wetter zu schlecht
Dem vierten kämpften die Soldaten nicht recht.
Vier Generäle
Und keiner kam an.

Sosso Robakidse
Marschierte nach Iran.
Er führte einen harten Krieg
Er hatte einen schnellen Sieg
Das Wetter war ihm gut genug
Und sein Soldat sich gut genug schlug.
Sosso Robakidse
Ist unser Mann.

From: Bertolt Brecht, *op.cit.*, pp. 40-41.

Four generals
Set out for Iran.
With the first one, war did not agree.
The second never won a victory.
For the third the weather never was right.
For the fourth the men would never fight.
Four generals
And not a single man!

Sosso Robakidse
Went marching to Iran

With him the war did so agree
He soon had won a victory.
For him the weather was always right.
For him the men would always fight.
Sosso Robakidse,
He is our man!

From: Eric Bentley, *op.cit.*, p. 120.

III

Ἀνάγκη νὰ σὲ πάρω ἐγὼ
Ποὺ ἔτσι σὲ παρατήσανε
Μονάχο κι᾿ ἔρμο κι᾿ ὀρφανό,
Παιδάκι μου, πῶς σὲ πονῶ.

Τὸ ροῦχο τὸ μεταξωτὸ
Μές᾿ τὸ ποτάμι τὄρριξα,
Φτωχὰ κουρέλια σοῦ φορῶ,
παιδάκι μου, πῶς σ᾿ ἀγαπῶ.

Δρόμο σὲ πῆρα, δρόμο μακρυνό,
Νυχτόμερα βαδίζοντας,
πείνασα καὶ ματώθηκα,
Μὰ νὰ σ᾿ ἀφήσω δὲν μπορῶ.

Σὲ μαῦρες μέρες καὶ σκληρές,
Πλένω σε καὶ βαφτίζω σε
Μέσ᾿ το κατάψυχρο νερό,
Μὴν κλαῖς καὶ μοῦ πικραίνεσαι.

Μάνος Χατζιδάκις, *Τέσσερα τραγούδια τοῦ Ὀδυσσέα Ἐλύτη ἀπὸ τὸν "Κύκλο μὲ τὴν Κιμωλία,"* (Manos Hadzidakis, *op.cit.*)

Da dich keiner nehmen will
Muss nun ich dich nehmen

Musst dich, da kein andrer war
Schwarzer Tag im magern Jahr
Halt mit mir bequemen.

Weil ich dich zu lang geschleppt
Und mit wunden Füssen
Weil die Milch so teuer war
Wurdest du mir lieb.
(Wollt dich nicht mehr missen.)
Werf dein feines Hemdlein weg
Wickle dich in Lumpen
Wasche dich und taufe dich
Mit dem Gletscherwasser.
(Musst es überstehen.)

From: Bertolt Brecht, *op.cit.*, p. 59.

Since no one else will take you, son,
I must take you.
Since no one else will take you, son,
You must take me.
O black day in a lean, lean year,
The trip was long, the milk was dear,
My legs are tired, my feet are sore:
But I wouldn't be without you any more.
I'll throw your silken shirt away
And dress you in rags and tatters.
I'll wash you, son, and christen you in glacier water.
We'll see it through together.

From: Eric Bentley, *op.cit.*, p. 128.

IV

Μιὰ φορὰ κι' ἕναν καιρὸ
Ζοῦσε ἕνα παιδὶ καλὸ

Ποὺ τὸ πότιζαν φαρμάκι,
Εἶχε μείνει ὀρφανό,
Δίχως φαΐ, δίχως νεράκι.

Παιδί, παιδάκι τῆς καρδιᾶς,
Παιδί, παιδάκι μου καρτέρα·
Κάποτε θάρθεῖ ἡ μέρα
Ὅπου θὰ φᾶς, ὅπου θὰ πιεῖς,
Κι᾽ ὅπου θὰ βρεῖς ἄλλη μητέρα.

Once upon a time
There lived a good child
They treated to poison;
He had been orphaned,
He had no food, he had no water.

Little child of the heart,
Little child of mine persevere;
Someday the day will come
When you shall eat, when you shall drink,
When you shall have another mother.

Μάνος Χατζιδάκις, *Τέσσερα τραγούδια τοῦ Ὀδυσσέα Ἐλύτη ἀπὸ τὸν "Κύκλο μὲ τὴν Κιμωλία,"* (Manos Hadzidakis, *op.cit.*) (Transl. by Stavros Deligiorgis)

Tief ist der Abgrund, Sohn
Brüchig der Steg
Aber wir wählen, Sohn
Nicht unsern Weg.

Musst den Weg gehen
Den ich weiss für dich
Musst das Brot essen
Das ich hab für dich.

Müssen die paar Bissen teilen
Kriegst von vieren drei
Aber ob sie gross sind
Weiss ich nicht dabei.

Dein Vater ist ein Räuber
Deine Mutter ist eine Hur
Und vor dir wird sich verbeugen
Der ehrlichste Mann.

Der Sohn des Tigers
Wird die kleinen Pferde füttern
Das Kind der Schlange
Bringt Milch zu den Müttern.

From: Bertolt Brecht, *op.cit.*, pp. 62-63.

Deep is the abyss, son,
I see the weak bridge sway
But it's not for us, son,
To choose the way.

The way I know
Is the one you must tread,
And all you will eat
Is my bit of bread.

Of every four pieces
You shall have three.
Would that I knew
How big they will be!

Your father is a bandit
A harlot the mother who bore you.

Yet honorable men
Shall kneel down before you.
Food to the baby horses
The tiger's son will take.
The mothers will get milk
From the son of the snake.

From: Eric Bentley, *op.cit.*, pp. 130-31.

V

Ἡ *πέτρα εἶν' ὁ θάνατος, ἡ πέτρα εἶν' ἡ ζωή μου·*
φυτρῶσαν ἄσπρα γιασεμιὰ μέσ' τὴν ἀναπνοή μου.
Εἶμ' ἕνα δέντρο ἔρημο, στὴν πέτρα σπάει ἡ φωνή μου·
Δέν μπαίνει ἀγέρας μήτε φῶς, πετρώνει τὸ κορμί μου.
Φέρτε κρασί, φέρτε φωτιὰ νὰ θάψω τὸν καημό μου.

Stone is death; stone is my life;
white jasmine has blossomed in my breath.
I am an abandoned tree, my voice breaks on stone;
no air, no light enters, my body turns to stone.
I am my mother's cry; I am the world's wound;
bring wine, bring fire that I may bury my woe.

Μάνος Χατζιδάκις, Ἀπόψε αὐτοσχεδιάζουμε (Manos Hadzidakis, *Apopse Aftoschediazoume*), Columbia, SEGG 2599 [Record]. (Trans. Stavros Deligiorgis)

VI

Φέρτε μου ἕνα μαντολίνο
Γιὰ νὰ δεῖτε πῶς πονῶ,
Κι' ὕστερα θὰ γίνω κρίνο,
Κι' ὕστερα πιὰ θὰ χαθῶ·

Τί μέ νοιάζει κι' ἄν χαθῶ
'Αφοῦ θἄχω γίνει κρίνο
Φέρτε μου ἕνα μαντολίνο.

Τὸ παιδὶ ποὺ μ'ἀγαπάει
῞Ολο θέλει νὰ ρωτᾶ
Τί σημαίνει Κυριακή·
Σκέφτομαι γιατὶ ρωτᾶ
Καὶ φοβᾶμαι πὼς ξεχνάει
Πὼς τὸν εἶδα Κυριακή.

Τὸ παιδὶ ποὺ μ'ἀγαπάει
῞Ολο θέλει νὰ ρωτᾶ
Ποῦ πηγαίνουν τὰ πουλιά·
Μὰ τὸ δάκρυ κυλάει
Καὶ καθὼς αὐτὸς κοιτᾶ
Τὸν σκεπάζω μὲ φιλιά.

Bring me a mandolin
And you'll see how I hurt,
Then I'll turn into a lily,
And then, at last, I'll vanish;
What do I care if I vanish
Since I will have turned into a lily
Bring me a mandolin.

The boy that loves me
Always likes to ask
What Sunday means;
I wonder why he asks
And I am afraid that he forgets
That I saw him one Sunday.

The boy that loves me
Always likes to ask

Where the birds go;
But my tears flow
And as he looks on
I cover him with kisses.

Μάνος Χατζιδάκις, Ἀπόψε αὐτοσχεδιάζουμε (Manos Hadzidakis, *op.cit*) (Trans. Stavros Deligiorgis)

VII

Ὁ ταχυδρόμος πέθανε.
Κι' ἦταν παιδὶ στὰ δεκαεφτὰ
ποὺ τώρα ἔχει πετάξει·
ποιὸς θὰ σοῦ φέρει, ἀγάπη μου, τὸ γράμμα ποὔχω τάξει;

Καὶ σὰν πουλὶ ποὺ πέταξε
ἡ πικραμένη του ζωὴ
πέταξε πάει καὶ τοὔφυγε ἡ δροσερὴ πνοή·
ποιὸς θὰ σοῦ δώσει, ἀγάπη μου, τὸ τελευταῖο φιλί μου;

Ὁ ταχυδρόμος πέθανε στὰ δεκαεφτά του χρόνια
κι' ἦταν αὐτὸς ἡ ἀγάπη μου·
ἡ κουρασμένη του σκιὰ τώρα πετᾶ στὰ κλώνια,
φέρνει δροσιὰ στ' ἀηδόνια.

Ποιὸς θὰ σοῦ δείξει, ἀγάπη μου, ποῦ εἶναι τ' ὀνείρου ὁ δρόμος
ἀφοῦ πεθάναμε μαζί, ἐγὼ κι' ὁ ταχυδρόμος.

The mailman is dead.
He was a kid of seventeen
that now has flown away;
who will bring you, my love, the letter that I've promised?

And like a bird that flew,
his saddened life

has flown, and his fresh breath is gone;
who will give you, my love, my last kiss?

The mailman died in his seventeenth year
and he was my love;
his tired shadow now flies in the boughs,
brings dew to the nightingales.

Who will show you, my love, where is the road of dreams
since we have died together, the mailman and I?

Μάνος Χατζιδάκις, *'Απόψε αὐτοσχεδιάζουμε* (Manos Hadzidakis, *op.cit*) (Trans. Stavros Deligiorgis)

Mario Vitti

9. *Family and Alienation in Contemporary Greek Fiction*

WE are all aware that the history of Greek fiction from 1920 to the present has still not been written. The studies we have at our disposal are often valuable and helpful, but they offer only fragmented aspects of the subject rather than a full, exhaustive survey. As often as not, we are dealing with book reviews, for example those brought together in Andreas Karandonis' *Πεζογράφοι καὶ πεζογραφήματα τῆς Γενιᾶς τοῦ* '30 (*Novelists and Novels of the Thirties*),[1] a collection of articles that this well-known critic published over an extended period—articles dealing with those novelists of his own generation who were of unquestioned importance. Indeed, his honesty in indicating the original date of each essay invites us to reflect more specifically upon the circumstances under which the essays were written. They are the impressions of a man who made the same journey as the novelists themselves; thus they witness to his own intellectual evolution.[2]

No matter how much of value a study of this kind may contribute, it cannot offer more than is permitted by the circumstances I have cited. We become even more aware of how inadequate it is for a broader judgment when we reflect upon the vast changes that have taken place in Greek fiction in the meantime—that is, since the last war. Young novelists, maturing in circumstances very different

[1] Athens, 1962.

[2] Karandonis confesses this himself: "I now see that this book of mine is nothing but the incidental passage of a critical sensibility through the authors and prose-works of, chiefly, our midwar period—works that happened to be the first to move that sensibility and often to shock it, or, in conformity with the psychology of that time, to fix enthusiasms in it that succeeded in displaying themselves more fully, whereas similar promptings concerning other authors remained merely unrealized plans" (*Ibid.*, p. 7).

from those existing for the writers of the Thirties, have created works that respond with immediacy to the demands of the new times. If we compare the two generations we shall be able to understand the degree to which these younger writers are tied to the immediate past, and in what ways they have assumed a contrary stance. Such a comparison will contribute not only to our investigation of the young writers' roots in the past, the sources of their experience; it will also help us to evaluate the work of the older writers. This is precisely my aim in this essay: to survey the postwar generation, and then, keeping in mind certain of its distinguishing features, to examine the "Generation of the Thirties" (I retain Theotokas' label for this group). The present essay cannot be exhaustive; it will merely suggest a point of view that, if acceptable, will hopefully be able to contribute to a more systematic study of the "Generation of the Thirties" and eventually to a critical evaluation of that generation.

The task that unfolds before an investigator with these intentions is a sufficiently extensive one. As an indication I shall note several topics that could lead to positive results. First and foremost, I am reminded of the enthusiasm for the spectacle of nature and life displayed by various novelists after the First World War. This contrasts to the indifference toward the natural environment on the part of the younger prose-writers. For the earlier novelists, to discover nature at that critical moment following the Asia Minor catastrophe was not an easy task. It came nevertheless as a natural reaction to the oppressive atmosphere of defeatism and inertia—an atmosphere that was not devoid, however, of cravings and expectations, as Angelos Terzakis has tried to remind us in a brief article whose pretext was the publication of Karyotakis' *Collected Works*.[3] Many of the young writers of this period felt an ardent need to deliver themselves from the heritage of a closed and oppressive environment. Not being able to take refuge in the outdoors as that outdoors had been stereotyped by the folklorist school—by the novelists of manners and morals—they tried the drastic solution of the *tabula rasa*. They greeted nature with a virgin glance. Fotis Kondoglou wrote in 1922: "The world before me is always fresh. . . . I listen intently to this splendid and sweet gurgling, my soul nourished by the austere, imperishable notes which sing away softly in the face of life's insignificant details."[4] Several years later, in 1930, Kosmas Politis published *The Lemon Grove*. Here, his joy in the created world is so great that he gives way to ecstatic ravings, with an enthusiasm that borders on the clumsy. The natural setting for his characters' actions is Poros; but it is also Delphi, Daphni, and the columns of the Temple of Olympian Zeus. He finds a new way by which the Greek novelist may confront his country's landscape, a landscape amalgamated now with archaeological sites.

For other writers, it was extreme violence that led to the discovery of nature: it was war in the trenches, as in Myrivilis' Ἡ Ζωὴ ἐν τάφῳ (*Life in the Tomb*).[5] This shattering experience affected Myrivilis decisively, liberat-

[3] Reprinted in Νέα Ἑστία, 81 (1967), 171-72. The same text, with slight changes, is also available in Terzakis' *Προσανατολισμὸς στὸν αἰῶνα* (*Orientation toward the Century*), Athens, 1963, pp. 191-94, dedicated to the poetess M. Polydouri.

[4] In Ὁ Λόγος (Constantinople), 4 (1922), p. 266.

[5] In the interests of historical accuracy let us not forget that the

ing him once and for all from the literary modes of the previous generation. Underground existence brought with it a new sense of nature intermixed with the longing for life. It is clear that writers of our own day have remained provokingly indifferent toward the discovery of life and of landscape, arriving finally at that pathological manifestation of indifference: alienation, even from all that pertains to nature.

Similarly, young writers have removed the discovery of life even from adolescence, which is the most natural period of discovery. Novels like Kosmas Politis' *Eroica* (1938) can no longer be written today, not only because today's writers lack the power to return to the childhood years by means of a lyrical or poetical mood, but also because adolescence itself, considered as a transitional period from childish innocence to adult knowledge and responsibility, is entirely missing from their lives. Spyros Plaskovitis, one of the recognized representatives of the postwar generation, reminds us of this in the following dramatic terms: "We were never either children or adolescents. It was as though we were born directly into adulthood; thus we began to view life awry, stripped of its stages."[6]

---

various sections of the book first appeared in the newspaper *Καμπάνα* of Mytilini, beginning with no. 1, April 10, 1923 and continuing to no. 41, January 29, 1924. Myrivilis' anti-war story "Τὸ *λουλοῦδι τῆς φωτιᾶς*" ("The Fire's Flower")—now collected in the volume Τὸ *κόκκινο βιβλίο* (*The Red Book*), Athens, 1953—appeared in the volume of the same title published in Lesbos in 1915 as "Τὸ *ἐθελοντικὸν*" ("The Volunteers"). Its first publication was in the periodical *Χαραυγὴ* (November 15, 1912).

[6] In the periodical *'Εποχές*, 45 (1966), 14.

Before I begin examining the subject that principally concerns me, I should like to suggest another direction that a comparative study of the two generations may effectively take: that of comparing the fictional dimensions—the area—of the earlier, seminal novelists such as Kosmas Politis, Theotokas, Terzakis, and Kastanakis, with the circumscribed area allowed us by the younger writers, who have insisted nightmarishly upon certain of life's circumstances and have willfully ignored its variety. These later writers have thus moved from the many-sided personalities of Theotokas' heroes, for example, to heroes who concentrate pathologically on only one facet of their being.

Closely interwoven with the topics I have just hastily sketched is another that I consider much more significant and that I shall therefore examine at closer hand. This involves one aspect of the more general topic which goes under the label "alienation." What are the features that indicate this phenomenon in the production of the recent generation? What conditions in the young novelists' experience have made them emerge alienated? These questions will help us not only to understand our contemporaries better, but also to gain a deeper view of a characteristic feature marking the production of the years between the two wars. In short, whereas the contemporary fictional hero is estranged from the social context—beginning with the family circle—the heroes of the previous generation of novelists lived and acted in the domestic environment, or took its presence for granted. More precisely, if the earlier novelist wished to discover the most genuine manifestations of his characters, he studied the relationships of those characters within the framework of the family. The postwar novelist perceived that family relationships had lost their genuineness, and he turned elsewhere in his search for his heroes' authenticity. This "elsewhere" begins just outside of the narrower domestic circle and leads to the ultimate consequence of definitive alienation—in other words, to the point at which human activity ceases to elicit a response from an *other*, and consequently ceases to be a *relationship*.

The young novelists did not push their characters to this extreme, but even at the point to which these characters were led, they display midwar Greece's social and intellectual condition with great faithfulness and responsibility. In order to apply the criterion I formulated at the start—i.e., in order to study the novels of the past generation while keeping in mind the condition of the present generation—I shall begin with the latter.

The war years created the background for the chief elements of ferment that ripened later. During these years the young writers confronted life for the first time, in the form in which it managed to present itself to them at that moment. There is no need for me to rehearse here the Resistance, the stance taken by Greek writers as a body, their faith in something better, something more honest—and the disillusion that came with the peace. In his Ἀ*ρνοῦμαι* (*I Refuse*), Andonis Samarakis, a representative figure of the new writing, makes one of his heroes cry out: "During the war I was certain of one thing: the world that would arrive after the war had ended. . . . That world was a certainty because I had come to believe—and who hadn't?—that it would come: a new, strangely different world . . . , one that would give both peace and bread to all mankind. . . . But it did not come."[7]

The consciousness of the young was formed in the period of war and Resistance, with its climate of unhesitating faith in man, and then in the period following the liberation, when people had to make the continually more difficult choice between one ideology and another. The Resistance, quite aside from everything else it represents in history, constitutes a landmark in the way everything pertaining to human relations was presented in fiction. In the works of the young writers—for example, in Nikos Kasdaglis' Τὰ *δόντια τῆς μυλόπετρας* (*The Millstone*) 1955, which treats Athenian resistance groups of opposing ideological orientation—we see the definitive impairment of the ancient institution of the family. The young fighters, released from the domestic environment, terrified at the thought of the death lying in wait for them at every street-corner, find their most genuine selves in a circle of contacts formerly unknown. This alteration in relationships, and the estrangement from the domestic hearth, continued in the years following the liberation; the change was irrevocable. Among the many examples we could offer is that of Margarita Liberaki, a young woman who, following in the footsteps of the prewar novel, had produced a refreshing story called Τὰ *ψάθινα καπέλα* (*The Straw Hats*), 1946, but who afterward wrote a condemnation of the family. This book, Ὁ *ἄλλος Ἀλέξανδρος* (*The Other Alexander*), 1950, presents two pairs of children borne to a single father by different mothers, and makes them confront each other with violence and hate. Each pair more-or-less knows the identity of the other two, yet

[7] 2nd edition, Athens, n.d. (1962), p. 192.

feels a corrosive attraction for them: Alexander and Aglaia sense something sick and murderous pulling them toward the other Alexander, the other Aglaia. In this fourfold interplay of fratricide and mutual annihilation, which tragically reflects the drama of the Civil War, we see the established institution of the family tottering irreparably.

Let us consider another woman, Galatia Sarandi. This gifted writer wished to give expression to our era by emphasizing the instinct for domestic security. While most of her contemporaries were struggling to express the ideological clash that characterizes our times, Sarandi wanted to avoid mentioning this clash—i.e., to accept it as a tacit assumption. In her final book, however, she gave way. The protagonist of Τὰ ὅρια (*The Boundaries*), 1966, is an unsatisfied man who defends himself sadistically and gratuitously against certain people while at the same time masochistically, and with equal gratuitousness, accepting the others' violence against him. He ends up in the hospital. Finally, after his discharge, he withdraws from the family (or rather from the simulacrum that his family has become) and, magnetized by something that surpasses common understanding, departs for a distant land that the narrator avoids naming.

In most cases the lost balance of family-based relationships could not be replaced by anything else. Little by little, isolation gave way to estrangement. Several writers whose time of military service was an experience of great intensity were inspired by this experience to write stories that are extremely suggestive. I would like to cite two very characteristic cases. The very title of Nikos Kasdaglis' Οἱ κεκαρμένοι (*Shaved Heads*), 1959, indicates the reduced individuality of the protagonists. (Let us not forget that shorn hair had a humiliating and punitive character not only in the Middle Ages but also in recent times in Europe, for example during the liberation period.) Kasdaglis' "shaved heads" act in the barracks, where their only bond is violence, hatred, and sexual rivalry. They cannot find a justification for their lives in this limited and artificial environment; surrounded by solitude, they discover only the denial of their selfhood. Contact with one's neighbor does not come by choice, but is imposed as a need that cannot be resisted. Alienation arises as the effect of mass guilt.[8]

The second story, Vassilis Vassilikos' T' *ἀγγέλιασμα* (*The Angel*), 1961, is not unknown to the American public.[9] Here, military life is presented in a metaphysical projection. Instead of treating this life realistically, Vasilikos transports us to an imaginary "School of Reserve Heavenly Angels" where the instructors' concern is to transform the recruits into higher beings absolutely obedient to regulations and entirely stripped of earthly, human feelings. In this journey toward deliverance from human experience, the Reserve Angel recollects his amatory adventures on earth as a final bond with life. The angel concludes his recital at the point in the instruction where his alienation from human existence has finally been almost completed. In the course of this recital he has recounted to us, without either enthusiasm or apparent protest, but with the most delicate irony, the trials through which he has passed.

[8] Kasdaglis undertook a more systematic account of the relation between institutionalized military service and the individual in his somewhat unsuccessful novel Ἐγὼ *εἰμὶ* Κύριος ὁ Θεός *σου* (*I Am the Lord Your Master*), Athens, 1961.

[9] See "Bibliographical Note," below.

Vassilikos has given us an additional depiction of alienation,[10] one employing a wealth of expressive means, in Τὸ *φύλλο* (*The Plant*), another story in his 1961 trilogy (see fn. 9). Here, a certain young man who has withdrawn into the solitude of an apartment, sees his alienation objectify and embody itself in a plant that grows and spreads until the entire home is invaded. If we ask ourselves what is the most decisive experience pushing a Greek toward this stance vis-à-vis society, we must answer: an extended period of spiritually repressive military service, precisely the type of service described by Vassilikos in Τ' *ἀγγέλιασμα* (*The Angel*). To carry this a step further, and to refer now to other writers besides Vassilikos: I believe that military service contributed decisively to the growth of alienation in postwar Greece, at least in literature. The country, after all, had lived through civil strife and the trials of guerrilla warfare; defense of its statehood had turned it into a despotic military-police organization. We should also remember that, however much this economically depressed country may constitute a market vied for by Western capital, it still has not reached the level of a society of consumers. It is therefore difficult to see how individual alienation can derive from a market economy that suffocates the individual.

In any case, we are strengthened in this view by the novels of the younger generation that come to mind—for example, Τὸ *λάθος* (*The Flaw*), 1965, by Andonis Samarakis, a recent novel that does not deal directly with the military yet shows us the consequences of a regime based

[10] Vassilikos took up this theme in one of the journalistic articles collected in his Ἐκτὸς *τῶν τειχῶν* (*Outside the Walls*), Athens, 1966.

on the army and the police. This book, which appeared in the United States in 1969,[11] presents a nameless man who lacks the credentials of a "good citizen" since he has not denounced anyone, and who has been arrested by two secret agents and brought to the capital to be interrogated. The novel's central subject is not precisely alienation; it is rather the relationship between the agents and the man they have arrested. But this terrified individual is more or less like the figures created by Samarakis in earlier books, figures who are isolated, without families, with doubtful pasts, and yet who, despite all this, do not intend to resign their need for communication—who do not, in short, wish to give way before the alienation threatening them. In Tὸ *λάθος*, the hero does not focus his attention on this problem. Yet, terrified as he is, he finds himself in the same situation as the man condemned to alienation, since the system rejects him. Here, alienation is caused by the state, just as it was by the military arm of the state in Kasdaglis and Vassilikos.

I could cite other examples of the abnormal relations between the individual and society, as these relations have been made vivid by young Greek novelists. The cases that I have already cited, however, are sufficient to sketch out the path the new generation has traveled toward this pathological tendency. The man who ceases to realize himself either within the family, or at least with the family still as something taken for granted, and who instead attempts to find his truest self among his comrades during the Resistance, this man—given the characteristics displayed by postwar society—alienates himself from his

[11] See "Bibliographical Note."

comrades as well, and is in danger of losing all possibility of human contact.

Today's crisis in human relationships offers the contemporary critic an experience that, from the methodological point of view, he would be remiss not to exploit if he is to examine works written between the two World Wars. Using the perspective that opens up before us, we may now study the relations between individual and society retrospectively and from this narrower viewpoint, in order to see man in his most immediate surroundings. To examine this subject in the output of the midwar period, we must inevitably isolate it from other, similar subjects with which it evolved side by side, which it influenced, and by which it was influenced. The few themes that we touched upon in our introductory material were intended to demonstrate precisely this. Though this method leads unavoidably to schematization, it will nevertheless help us to distinguish certain ingredients effectively.

George Theotokas' novel Ἀργὼ (*Argo*), 1936, for example, involves a multitude of elements besides the one that interests us at the moment; it is a novel about people who are perfectly integrated into society, and one in which the domestic web plays an appropriate role. Writing at a time when Greek novelists were more or less turning their attention to family histories (cf. Terzakis in Ἡ *παρακμὴ τῶν Σκληρῶν* [*The Decline of the Skliri*], 1932; Kastanakis in Ἡ *φυλὴ τῶν ἀνθρώπων* [*The Human Race*], 1932; P. Floros in Ἄποικοι [*The Colonists*], 1934; Petsalis in Ὁ *ἀπόγονος* [*The Descendant*], 1935), Theotokas likewise tried to declare something when he used the history of a family, "An academic dynasty," as the prologue to his plot. In this intentionally decentralized novel, with its scores of characters, Theotokas not only wished to note the family background of each of his personages with utmost care; he also used the family as an element in the design of his story's interlocking events.

Theotokas' aim was no doubt more encompassing than this; he hoped to cover the greatest possible number of ways that man's life in society manifests itself. Moreover, he conceived of the novelistic genre as one whose "development admits of no limitations."[12] On the other hand, the most burning question that Theotokas always wished to answer by fictional means was whether justice exists in this world and what masks it dons in politics, friendship, love—even in everyday activities within the home. Given the variety of manifestations that Theotokas wished to encompass, it was to be expected that his characters' moral development should be realized most often in dealings that could take place only outside the family.

Of the novelists who concentrated their attention and concern on the individual's behavior within the closed and oppressive environment of the family, Angelos Terzakis is one whom we must note especially. This is not simply because of the quality of his works. Our attention should focus upon those of his books which go beyond the conventional family and attempt experimentation. We should focus, for example, not so much on *The Decline of the Skliri* (1932) or on Ἡ *μενεξεδένια πολιτεία* (*Purple City*), 1937, as on *Στοργὴ* (*Tenderness*), 1944. Here, Terzakis creates an artificial family. A man who is somewhat of a drifter decides to cohabit with a young woman

[12] Ἐποχές, 20 (1964), 9.

and her daughter, and to assume the responsibilities of the husband who has abandoned her. The author subjects his hero to great trials within this domestic web and attempts to survey the steadfastness of certain feelings—of tenderness itself, for example. In his novel Δίχως Θεὸ (*Without God*), written more recently (1951), Terzakis attempted once more to fashion an artificial family. In this case a bachelor adopts two nephews. Inspired by Marxist ideas, the middle-aged protagonist hopes to produce "two strong, free people" (p. 101). The end result is that he dies with the knowledge that he has failed, and without even the consolation of faith in God. By means of these experimental families, Terzakis pushed a basic theme to the extreme limit of its evolution, yoking it to urgent problems connected with education and with a political orientation continually more difficult in our times.

In conclusion, I would say that although the family as an area of sociological investigation naturally was not discovered by the generation of the Thirties, yet a concern felt by previous generations was brought to maturity by these writers, who enriched it with daring psychological probings and a wealth of themes, as we have seen in the cases of Theotokas and Terzakis. Let us not forget that this maturity coincided with a splendid current of creativity that bequeathed to the Greek novel a new, virgin awareness of the world, and seemed thereby to decrease the distance that until then had separated Greek fiction from its Western counterpart in this regard. Subsequent developments, hastened by the war, came like a natural expansion of this situation. Neither earlier nor later did

Greek writers falsify the social and spiritual state of their land in order to apply formulas originating in the West. It is true that Kafka and Camus in recent times, like Dostoevsky previously (to mention only the greatest names), functioned as instruments spreading open new angles of vision. The fact, however, that the new novels were generated from the life of Greek society, and indeed in some cases from experiences foreign to the West,[13] is an indisputable guarantee of their authenticity.

Bibliographical Note

Of the writers of the thirties who have commented upon the novelists of their own generation, I wish to mention, in addition to A. Karandonis, the following: *Πέτρος Χάρης* (*Ἕλληνες πεζογράφοι*, 3 vols.), *Ἄλκης Θρύλος* (*Μορφὲς τῆς ἑλληνικῆς πεζογραφίας*, 2 vols.), and the much more methodical I. M. *Παναγιωτόπουλος* (vol. 2 of the series *Τὰ πρόσωπα καὶ τὰ κείμενα*, Athens, 1943). A younger critic, A. *Σαχίνης*, has devoted himself exclusively to studying the modern Greek novel. I would single out his *Ἡ σύγχρονη πεζογραφία μας*, Athens, 1951, and *Τό νεοελληνικὸ μυθιστόρημα*, Athens, 1958. This critic, who is the one and only person, so far as I know, who teaches the subject from a professorial chair (at Salonica), has brought together his book reviews of the recent generation in the volume *Νέοι πεζογράφοι* (1945-1965), Athens, 1965. It is to this unique book, which is practically a panoramic inventory, that I would refer the reader who desires a complete picture of the present generation of Greek writers.

[13] For example, precisely the fact of alienation arising out of military service.

Of the novels and stories cited, the following are obtainable in English translation: Margarita Liberaki, *The Other Alexander*, tr. W. and H. Tzalopoulou Barnstone, N.Y., Noonday Press, 1959; Vassilis Vassilikos, *The Plant, the Well, the Angel*, tr. Edmund and Mary Keeley, N.Y., Knopf, 1964; A. Samarakis, *The Flaw*, tr. P. Mansfield and R. Burns, N.Y., Weybright and Talley, 1969; G. Theotokas, *Argo*, tr. Margaret Brooke and A. Tsatsopoulos, London, Methuen, 1951. The writer of the present essay treats the same subject (in a historical perspective) in chapters 14 and 16 of his *Storia della letteratura neogreca* (Turin, 1971).

C. Th. Dimaras

10. *Survivances du romantisme dans la culture néo-hellénique*

LA PÉRIODISATION dans le domaine des sciences diachroniques est, sans doute, en premier lieu une exigence de notre esprit, dans son effort pour donner un sens au déroulement de l'histoire. Toutefois, si une certaine supposition que j'ai avancée naguère à ce sujet n'est pas tout à fait sans fondement, la matière de nos études imposerait, elle aussi, la notion d'unités successives qui marqueraient leur présence dans le déroulement du temps. D'ailleurs, si, l'homme restant inchangé tant que nous en suivons les traces dans son histoire, ses manifestations se modifient, il faut bien rechercher la cause de ces changements ailleurs que dans une évolution qui n'est pas détectable en ce qui concerne le temps historique. L'explication que j'ai proposée là-dessus fait appel à deux idées qui, réellement, sont très proches l'une de l'autre. Premièrement, à chaque nouveau mouvement culturel, l'excipient humain qui lui sert de véhicule appartient à un type humain différent de celui qui a assuré le mouvement précédent. En second lieu, les modifications dont nous nous occupons ici consistent en changements de densité de certains éléments; elles sont quantitatives: à partir du moment où le nombre des éléments en question devient assez grand pour donner à la culture un coloris particulier, nous avons affaire à une nouvelle période.[1]

Ainsi, non seulement la période devient une entité dont

[1] Il me semble peu séant de charger ce bref exposé de notes élaborées. Qu'il me soit permis, une fois pour toutes, de renvoyer le lecteur à un petit volume paru en 1969 à Genève, sous le titre *La Grèce au temps des Lumières*, où j'ai réuni quelques-uns de mes travaux antérieurs concernant des problèmes homocentriques à ceux qui sont traités ici. D'autre part, l'usager pourra consulter pour les réalia de ces mêmes sujets mon *Histoire de la littérature néo-hellénique*, Athènes, 1965 (et Annexe, 1966).

l'approche peut être objectivée, et qui correspond à une réalité essentielle, forcément nécessaire à l'étude, mais elle prend une importance particulière par le fait qu'elle permet l'examen du comportement des types humains stables devant des appels divers. Ce second point ne retiendra pas notre attention dans le cas particulier qui nous intéresse aujourd'hui; mais qu'il me soit permis d'insister sur un corollaire de ce que je viens d'avancer; à savoir sur l'importance des transitions dans l'étude de l'histoire culturelle: si je suis dans le vrai, il n'y a pas de commencement, il n'y a pas de fin dans le développement de la vie culturelle d'une nation. Il n'y a que des changements de proportions entre le futur qui sera un jour l'actuel, mais qui déjà y est présent, et l'actuel qui sera un jour le passé, mais sans, par cela, cesser complètement d'agir. Quoi qu'en disent les auteurs de manifestes, il n'y a jamais, sauf pour des causes extérieures, rupture de continuité dans la vie culturelle: qui veut bien connaître un mouvement trouvera son profit à étudier aussi bien les antécédents de celui-ci que ses survivances; ceci est une vérité ancienne, certes, mais empirique. Enfin il me faudra revenir sur un détail important dans ce domaine: les éléments empruntés par une période à une autre peuvent être utilisés à des fins qui sont sans rapport avec leur destination initiale, ou qui, même, lui sont contraires.

Tout cela étant dit, il me semble opportun de nous introduire maintenant dans le champ des applications, en étudiant une région particulièrement inexplorée de cette aire généralement peu connue qu'est la culture néohellénique: nous allons méditer sur l'existence et sur le sort de quelques éléments qui, considérés comme typiquement romantiques dans le développement du romantisme néo-hellénique, ont survécu à celui-ci et sont présents et actifs dans la vie culturelle de la Grèce contemporaine. Les dates que nous allons adopter pour ce faire sont, si je ne me trompe, généralement admises dans l'histoire littéraire néo-hellénique: le mouvement débuterait vers 1830, pour se terminer vers 1880; un grand nombre d'événements, de faits, de manifestations, convergent autour de ces dates pour leur donner une valeur satisfaisante. Remarquons, en passant, que ces bornes situent le romantisme hellénique un peu en aval de ses homologues occidentaux, ce qui est tout à fait régulier, compte tenu du décalage généralement existant entre le développement des cultures occidentales et celui de la culture néo-hellénique, laquelle, juste durant cette époque, tâche de se mettre au pas avec celles-ci.

Nous n'avons pas à nous occuper ici de la première des deux dates; quant à la seconde, il est peut-être opportun de rappeler que les années '80 ont été précédées par une décennie durant laquelle l'équipe littéraire en poste avait été décimée par la mort. En 1868, P. Soutzo, le survivant des deux frères, était mort; il est suivi dans la tombe par J. Carassoutza (1873) et par D. Paparrigopoulos (1873); une année plus tard, c'est le tour de Sp. Vassiliadis. Lorsque Aristote Valaoritis meurt en 1879, il ne reste plus qu'Achille Paraschos comme poète représentatif de son temps. Ceci, dans une culture encore axée sur le lyrisme, et une population littéraire peu nombreuse, créait des conditions particulièrement favorables à l'éclosion d'une nouvelle génération poétique; c'est ce qui eut lieu: dès 1880 trois jeunes poètes—N. Campas, C. Coccos et G. Drossinis—publient à quelques mois d'écart leurs premières plaquettes de vers, dans un esprit foncièrement différent de ce qui avait précédé: la légèreté enjouée à la place du sombre pessimisme, le sotto-voce galant à la place de l'emphase abstraite, Heine et François Coppée détrônant Hugo et Lamartine. La même année, une traduction de *Nana*, publiée en volume, provoque une sensation frisant le scandale. Voilà ce que l'on peut appeler densité de phénomènes dans l'ordre de la culture. Costis Palamas, dont par hasard le nom ne figura pas à cette première promotion, publiait alors des vers du même genre dans les journaux de l'époque; son premier recueil, dans un esprit identique, paraîtra en 1886. En 1888 Psichari va publier son *Voyage*, dont la prose apporte un élément nouveau, non seulement quant à la langue, mais aussi en ce qui concerne l'intimité du ton.

Mon père avait vingt-huit ans à la fin du siècle; ma famille et mes maîtres m'enseignèrent que là, dans cette profonde entaille de 1880, une ère nouvelle avait commencé pour la Grèce, que la volonté de progrès, de renouveau, s'était fait jour, en repoussant dans le passé les formules périmées du romantisme. Et cela, comme de juste, était valable non seulement en ce qui concernait les lettres ou la culture, mais aussi pour la politique, pour la doctrine. Nous l'avons cru pendant longtemps. La génération qui avait succédé à celle de 1880, préoccupée beaucoup plus par l'action que par la recherche historique, avait tendance à insister sur l'originalité des nouvelles formations, et d'ignorer les liens qui unissaient celles-ci au passé: le romantisme repoussé par le naturalisme, le langage factice du purisme remplacé par le réalisme linguistique du parler populaire, la fameuse grande idée des politiciens romantiques cédant à la poussée de la politique positive. Cela est à peu près le schéma du développement historique de la Grèce tel qu'il nous a été enseigné par nos pères.

Pourtant, depuis longtemps déjà, la Grèce s'est mise à la recherche historique, approfondit son passé immédiat, découvre, compare. Nous avons par rapport à ce qu'en savaient nos maîtres, une notion beaucoup plus détaillée de ce que fut le romantisme grec dans ses différentes expressions. Je n'en ferai pas ici l'inventaire; il me suffira d'en retrouver plus loin les éléments qui auront été nécessaires à notre exposé et d'en indiquer l'importance relative. Pour cela, il ne faudra pas oublier que la Grèce est par excellence une de ces nations qu'un mot heureux a qualifiées de romantiques:[2] chez d'autres peuples, les passages au classicisme ou de celui-ci au romantisme exprimaient simplement les étapes d'un développement régulier de leur histoire; chez les Hellènes se trouvant dans les situations correspondantes, il s'agissait d'éléments constitutifs de leur risorgimento.

Or, tâchons de dénombrer ces changements dont se vantaient nos pères. Il y eut, d'abord, et il ne faut pas en minimiser l'importance, la campagne linguistique, la tentative, qui ne fut pas infructueuse, de ramener le langage écrit aussi près que possible de la langue parlée, populaire. Il y eut, en poésie, l'abandon de certaines formules romantique bouffies et l'adoption de formes poétiques proches de la tradition des chansons folkloriques. Enfin nous devons signaler aussi le développement de la prose d'imagination, nous pourrions presque

[2] Je me réfère ou titre du livre d'Etienne Fournol, *Les nations romantiques* (Paris 1931), en lui donnant peut-être un sens un peu plus restreint que celui qu'il a dans la pensée de l'auteur.

dire son avènement en ce qui concerne l'actualité littéraire grecque. La prose des années 1880, dont celle de nos jours descend directement, s'inspire des tendances naturalistes et se crée par cela un genre particulier, la description des moeurs villageoises, ce qui a reçu un nom dans le vocabulaire littéraire de la langue grecque, l'*éthographie*; de celle-ci, l'urbanisation progressant, a découlé la description des moeurs de la petite bourgeoisie. Inutile de dire qu'en tout cela les influences étrangères sont toujours détectables, et que les parallèles sont faciles à établir; mais nous savons tous maintenant que, pour qu'une influence soit viable (et telle est la caractéristique des phénomènes que nous groupons ici), il faut qu'elle corresponde à des exigences, à des besoins profonds, du sujet récepteur.

Si dans les trois exemples qui précèdent nous semblons avoir signalé des expressions essentielles de la culture néo-hellénique, il serait, sans doute, opportun d'élargir encore le champ de notre expérience et de dépasser nettement le domaine littéraire. Cela a déjà été fait dans le cas de la langue, sujet qui couvre une partie de la littérature, mais qui s'étend aussi sur toutes les autres émanations de l'activité sociale. Néanmoins il y a deux autres manifestations de la conscience néo-hellénique qui méritent d'être citées ici. Dans le domaine des sciences, l'une a été crue complètement indigène, issue d'exigences locales, indépendamment de toute autre activité parallèle occidentale: la discipline folklorique; pour cette raison, il est nécessaire de l'étudier ici en tant que ressortissant à la pensée néo-hellénique. Enfin, pour éviter des exemples difficiles à développer dans une réunion qui s'occupe d'histoire culturelle, il en est un qui, appartenant à la pensée politique, correspond aussi à un des éléments les plus profonds de la conscience nationale grecque: l'idée que le peuple grec a une mission à remplir dans le monde. Nous pouvons retenir cette opinion comme une des plus fondamentales de notre enquête: si vous arrêtez l'homme de la rue à Athènes et que vous lui dites que le peuple grec n'a aucune mission à remplir dans le monde, qu'aucun peuple n'a aucune mission à remplir, il est fort probable qu'il vous taxera d'ignorance ou d'imbécillité; ces choses-là ne sont pas à discuter, elles sont censées être acceptées à l'unanimité. Ainsi le concept de mission des peuples, éminemment romantique, se retrouve, dans ces conditions, actuel et agissant.

Donc, nous avons réuni au total cinq éléments, à titre d'échantillons, mais dont l'importance absolue ou par rapport à la Grèce est certaine. Il ne me paraît pas impossible de les ramener à un dénominateur commun, qui en dernière analyse n'est autre que le romantisme lui-même. Si cela n'est pas entièrement faux, il nous faudra reconnaître que la vie culturelle grecque est régie par le romantisme.

Néanmoins, nous pouvons étudier la question de plus près. Cette idée de mission sur laquelle nous avons finalement débouché nous rapproche des deux philosophies qui ont annoncé la pensée, la biosophie romantique: j'ai cité la philosophie de Vico et celle de Herder. Cette vision du peuple porteur d'un mandat inaliénable dans l'histoire de l'humanité par la grâce de ses qualités particulières, comporte, avec la notion supplémentaire de pureté originelle, celle de la langue, des moeurs, des institutions, des émanations artistiques, toutes expressions qui doivent être étudiées et approfondies si nous voulons connaître ce peuple. D'autre part, le retour aux formes initiales constitue dans ces conditions une garantie de pureté, et, par conséquent, d'efficacité que recherchera quiconque croit à la mission des peuples.

Ainsi, nous le savions déjà (mais l'application n'en a pas été faite de façon suffisante en ce qui concerne notre sujet), des manifestations de curosité autour de l'histoire, de la langue et du folklore de chaque unité nationale sont apparentées étroitement à l'enseignement ou aux conséquences de l'enseignement vichien ou herderien. Cela n'exclut pas la possibilité qu'il y ait d'autres causes qui pressent dans le même sens; nous avons même de bonnes raisons pour croire *a priori* que cette éventualité est la plus probable. Mais ce qui nous intéresse ici, c'est de constater que, dans le domaine de la culture, trois des manifestations les plus essentielles de la Grèce moderne ont leurs racines profondes dans ce qui a créé le romantisme, et même, pour aller un peu plus loin, dans ce qu'a été le romantisme.

Il existe une doctrine officielle grecque, formée à l'encontre des vues historiques de Gibbon: non seulement l'histoire du peuple hellène est une, mais le lien qui unit l'histoire grecque ancienne à l'histoire grecque moderne n'est autre que l'empire byzantin. Or, jusqu'à un temps assez proche, la première partie de cette affirmation n'avait pas été mise en doute: pour louer les descendants ou pour les dénigrer par des comparaisons simplistes, pratiquement tous ceux qui s'occupaient de la question, s'accordaient à faire descendre la Grèce moderne de la Grèce antique. Cela jusqu'au moment où un savant allemand,

Fallmerayer, avança une thèse différente; les faits sont trop connus pour qu'il y ait lieu de s'y étendre. Mais ce peuple, fatigué par une longue guerre, déçu par les résultats acquis, ayant déjà perçu les appels romantiques, vit le danger, saisit avec perspicacité et selon l'air du temps, les éléments de la riposte: au fond des premières réclamations, nous voyons déjà se profiler le nouveau visage de la Grèce, tel que doit le présenter un historien romantique de génie, Constantin Paparrigopoulos: non seulement l'unité était sauvegardée, mais l'empire byzantin était rétabli à sa place, chaînon solide entre l'antiquité et le monde moderne.

Inutile d'insister sur le caractère romantique de cette doctrine, qui puisait sa puissance dans la volonté nationale et son schéma dialectique dans la réhabilitation du moyen âge.[3] Mais nous avons cité aussi la langue. L'opinion établie veut que, répondant à un néo-classicisme dû à des causes multiples, les intellectuels qui ont réagi au romantisme aient fait preuve d'esprit progressiste et positif en préconisant l'usage généralisé du langage populaire. Naturellement la réalité est infiniment plus nuancée; il y eut, bien entendu, au siècle des Lumières, une poussée

[3] Fait significatif: un terme forgé au plus fort du romantisme hellène, en 1852, par un interprète hautement représentatif de l'historicisme romantique grec, Sp. Zampélios, le mot *helléno-chrétien*, a été introduit de notre temps, exactement un siècle plus tard, dans le vocabulaire de la Constitution (1952). Ainsi, loin de pouvoir enregistrer une sécularisation progressive, une opinion soutenue encore récemment, nous assistons à une cléricalisation graduelle conforme à l'esprit du romantisme grec; et ceci après la fin de la période romantique. Quant à la notion d'unité, diachronique et synchronique (latente ou explicite dans plusieurs autres expressions nationales du mouvement romantique), il se pourrait qu'elle fût la plus caractéristique du romantisme grec.

dans ce sens: là il peut être question d'esprit positif et éclairé. Mais à l'apogée du romantisme, si, d'une part, la volonté d'affirmer une descendance contestée conduisait à une tentative de résurrection du grec ancien, d'autre part l'exaltation de la notion du peuple impliquait aussi la promotion de la langue populaire. Ce parallèle n'est pas seulement sensible chez un poète, comme Solomos, mais nous pouvons le détecter chez les représentants théoriques du renouveau de 1880; le mouvement qui pousse à l'adoption de la langue démotique a diverses causes, dont il ne faut pas exclure le populisme et l'historicisme romantique, ni en diminuer l'importance.

D'ailleurs, une autre voie qui s'ouvre à notre réflexion nous mènerait à la même constatation: le folklore, qui commence à prendre forme pendant la période romantique, et dans les mêmes conditions, exactement, que l'historicisme, est une émanation directe de l'esprit de Herder, ou de Vico, selon le cas, tel que l'a appliqué le romantisme. La discipline qui a donné au monde grec ce qu'il possède de plus riche dans l'ordre de la recherche, est née d'une envolée romantique, mais a surtout proliféré à partir de la fin du romantisme et jusqu'à nos jours avec une constance impressionnante. Là, dans cet ensemble, nous retrouverons la langue populaire, expression, par sa pureté, de la pure âme populaire, mais nous retrouverons aussi autre chose, à savoir: la chanson populaire et la vie sociale des simples.

La chanson devait encourager les tendances contraires au langage savant, puisqu'elle ne s'exprime que dans la langue commune, mais en même temps favoriser la nouvelle poésie, qui se refusait à la grandiloquence des poètes romantiques et recherchait la simplicité, la naïveté. Cela se fit d'autant plus facilement que la nouvelle génération se manifesta surtout dans le lyrisme;[1] mais indépendamment de ce fait, on peut dire qu'une grande proportion de la poésie post-romantique imite la chanson populaire ou s'en inspire. Quant à l'intérêt porté aux moeurs des simples, où nous retrouvons le jeu double de l'amour qui conduit au sujet, et du sujet qui inspire l'amour, s'il s'est manifesté pendant la période romantique, comme matière d'études et prétexte d'amplifications oratoires, certes il se trouve en même temps à la base du naturalisme que l'on a cru pouvoir opposer au mouvement romantique. Or le naturalisme est non seulement l'élément le plus nouveau qu'ait apporté la génération de 1880, mais continue de nos jours à exprimer l'essentiel de la prose néo-hellénique, pour autant qu'elle n'a pas assimilé les formules du modernisme. Loin de constituer des désaveux du romantisme, la promotion de la langue démotique, l'inspiration tirée de la chanson populaire et mise à profit par la poésie savante, l'étude et la description des moeurs des simples sont des continuations de celui-ci.

Ainsi, il semble que nous pouvons affirmer sans exagération deux faits qui se complètent pour donner à

[1] Pour ce qui est du lyrisme tel que nous le comprenons de nos jours, je suis prêt à m'accorder avec ceux d'entre nous qui considèrent qu'il constitue un apport du romantisme. Ceci vaut même pour les excès du modernisme le plus outré en poésie. Dans ces conditions, l'exemple n'aurait pas une valeur spécifiquement grecque en ce qui concerne la survivance du romantisme. Mais il ne cesserait pas pour autant d'être valable quant à la Grèce aussi. D'ailleurs, en admettant une généralisation de ce genre, on est astreint simultanément à ne pas perdre de vue les causes multiples qui se joignent pour aboutir à un même effet.

notre argumentation un maximum de poids: d'une part, des éléments fondamentaux du romantisme grec se sont introduits dans la culture post-romantique, et, d'autre part, des éléments importants de la culture post-romantique sont bel et bien des survivances du romantisme. Le passage qui s'effectue du romantisme à la période suivante, laquelle est communément désignée par un de ses aspects les plus caractéristiques, le naturalisme, ne peut plus être considéré comme un changement qualitatif, mais simplement comme une variation de densité, de degré.

Reste à savoir en premier lieu si, à côté de causes qui seraient généralement valables, il y en aurait d'autres spécifiquement grecques, qui, elles, exigeraient une étude particulière. Là il faut admettre que l'élément local est très nettement perceptible. La Grèce est née à une heureuse conjoncture du néo-classicisme et du romantisme. Cela fut une des causes auxiliaires du retard que nous constatons quant aux infiltrations romantiques dans la culture néo-hellénique; mais ce qui fut plus important encore, comme résultat de cette rencontre, c'est le fait que certains éléments du néo-classicisme se mélangèrent au mouvement romantique et donnèrent ainsi au romantisme grec son caractère particulier, national. A partir de là, ce corps hybride du romantisme hellène restait ouvert à diverses pressions et s'offrait sans difficulté à des mélanges nouveaux. D'autre part, et dans un sens contraire, on pourrait supposer que ce retard, ce décalage, donnait plus de force au mouvement sortant, le romantisme en l'occurrence, par conséquent plus de résistance, ce qui lui permit de laisser plus de traces dans la nouvelle formation culturelle. Enfin, "not least," il ne faut jamais oublier lorsque nous traitons de cette question, combien profonde, et comme attendue, a été la poussée romantique dans la vie hellène: partant de là, nous devons nous attendre à retrouver partout, lorsque nous explorons la culture grecque moderne, des éléments romantiques.

Reste à savoir, et c'est par cette observation que je me permets de clore mon rapport, reste à savoir si l'acceptation des matériaux du romantisme par les représentants des mouvements qui le suivirent se fit dans un esprit romantique, ou, plus profondément encore, se fit consciemment. Là, dès le début, nous avons constaté que le naturalisme grec, et tout ce qui s'ensuivit, fit du romantisme sans le savoir, et plus encore, en le méprisant. Mais un des plaisirs les plus aigus de nos recherches consiste à détecter les voies subtiles que suit le devenir historique faisant feu de tout bois, profitant de tous les éléments du passé, les plus disparates, les plus contradictoires, pour vivifier chaque fois le présent. En fin de compte, les idées seraient bien peu de chose dans l'ensemble de la vie et de la conscience humaine: on dirait que c'est plutôt l'affectivité qui domine dans le champ de l'histoire.

Notes on the Contributors

Zissimos Lorenzatos is a poet and critic living in Kifissia. His books include Ἡμερολόγιο (*Diary*), Μικρὰ Σύρτις (*Syrtis Minor*), and Μελέτες (*Studies*). He has also translated Pound's *Cathay* poems and William Blake's *The Marriage of Heaven and Hell.*

Angelos Terzakis is a prolific novelist, dramatist, and critic of the theatre. Among his best known works are Πριγκηπέσσα Ἰζαμπὼ (*Princess Izabeau*), Δίχως Θεὸ (*Without God*), and Μυστικὴ Ζωὴ (*Secret Life*). He is also a teacher of drama at the School of Drama of the National Theatre, and a regular contributor to the newspaper Τὸ Βῆμα.

Bertrand Bouvier is director of studies in modern Greek language and literature at the University of Geneva. He has published scholarly work on the history of ancient Greek drama, on Byzantine art, and on modern Greek folklore and poetry.

Thanasis Maskaleris is Assistant Professor of Comparative Literature and Creative Writing at San Francisco State College. He has published poems, translations, and critical studies in the field of modern Greek literature, and he is preparing a study of Palamas for the Twayne World Authors Series.

Edmund Keeley is Professor of English and Creative Arts at Princeton University, and President of the Modern Greek Studies Association. He has published four novels set in Greece. His editions and translations include *Six Poets of Modern Greece, George Seferis: Collected Poems,*

1924-1955 and *C. P. Cavafy: Selected Poems* (with Philip Sherrard); *Vassilis Vassilikos: The Plant, The Well, The Angel* (with Mary Keeley); and *C. P. Cavafy: Passions and Ancient Days* (with George Savidis).

PETER BIEN is Professor of English at Dartmouth College, and former Secretary of the Modern Greek Studies Association. His books include a study of L. P. Hartley, a critical monograph on Cavafy, several translations of Kazantzakis, and most recently, *Kazantzakis and the Linguistic Revolution in Greek Literature.*

PETER LEVI, S.J., is a classical tutor at Campion Hall, Oxford. He has published several books of poems, an edition of Pausanias, and was editor of the special issue of *Agenda* devoted to modern Greek literature.

STAVROS DELIGIORGIS is Associate Professor of English and Comparative Literature at the University of Iowa. He has written a number of scholarly articles in the field of Greek literature, among these "Boccaccio and the Greek Romances" and "Fauriel and Modern Greek Poetry." He has also translated Wellek and Warren's *Theory of Literature* into Greek.

MARIO VITTI is Professor of modern Greek literature at the University of Palermo, Italy. His publications include several standard editions of Greek poets in Italian translation, an anthology of contemporary Greek poetry, an edition of Calvos' work in Italian, and a history of modern Greek literature.

C. Th. Dimaras, Director of the Neo-hellenic Research Center of the National Hellenic Research Foundation in Athens, has recently been appointed Professor, and Directeur de l'Institut Néo-Hellénique, at the Sorbonne. His many publications include *Ἱστορία τῆς νεοελληνικῆς λογοτεχνίας* (*History of Modern Greek Literature*), *Δύο φίλοι, Κοραῆς καὶ Βάμβας* (*Two Friends: Korais and Vamvas*), Ὁ *ἑλληνικὸς Διαφωτισμὸς* (*The Greek Enlightenment*), and *La Grèce au temps des Lumières.*

Index